# FAITH THAT GOES THE DISTANCE

*Living an* Extraordinary *Life*

# JUD WILHITE

## Baker Books

A Division of Baker Book House Co
Grand Rapids, Michigan 49516

Published by Baker Books
a division of Baker Book House Company
P.O. Box 6287, Grand Rapids, MI 49516-6287

Printed in the United States of America

**Library of Congress Cataloging-in-Publication Data**

Wilhite, Jud, 1971–
    Faith that goes the distance : living an extraordinary life / Jud Wilhite.
        p.      cm.
    Includes bibliographical references.
    ISBN 0-8010-1237-6 (pbk.)
        1. Faith.  2. Faith—Biblical teaching.  3. Bible. N.T. Hebrews XI—Criticism, interpretation, etc.  I. Title.
    BV4637 .W49 2002
    234'.23—dc21                         2002001940

For current information about all releases from Baker Book House, visit our web site:
                  http://www.bakerbooks.com

# FAITH THAT GOES THE DISTANCE

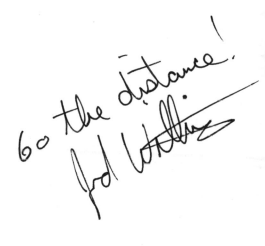

Go the distance!

To Emma
May your faith
carry you the distance

# CONTENTS

# ACKNOWLEDGMENTS

Faith is a verb, suggests Kathleen Norris. And in this case it is also a noun, a preposition, and an adjective, among other things. The faith of many people carried this book when my own faith wavered. I am grateful to Guy Greenfield for his confidence. Thanks to Vicki Crumpton, my editor, and the awesome team at Baker for taking this project the distance. I appreciate those who read all or part of the manuscript, especially Clarice Cassada, Regi Fowler, Geoff Johnson, John Ketchen, Dianna Melson, Scott Schlotfelt, Carolyn Williams, and Shawn Williams. To those whose stories are contained in these pages, thank you for opening your lives and sharing honestly. To Barry McMurtrie, thanks for your friendship and leadership. To my wife, Lori, I can't thank you enough for your encouragement, love, support, and faith. And thanks to Emma, my daughter, who inspires me and reminds me of God's faithfulness.

# Introduction

*In some people religion exists as a dull habit, in others
as an acute fever.*[1]

WILLIAM JAMES

Three o'clock in the morning. I had escaped a group
of armed attackers, declined a nomination to be president of the United States, and sailed smooth waters on a
sleek sailboat with my wife. Things seemed beautiful—
until a deafening sound crashed into my dream world.

The sound's volume paralyzed me. Was it the fire alarm?
Were nuclear bombs falling from the sky? Was it the last
trumpet at Jesus' second coming? My eyes opened. I jumped
up and scurried to find clothes. I hopped through the living room, pulling up my jeans, jerked the front door open,
and ran into the freezing night.

Everything was dark. I saw no fire; no bombs fell from the
sky. And if Jesus had returned, nobody on my block seemed
aware. But there was one problem—our '92 Grand Am sat
in the driveway with the horn blaring. The odd thing was

that the car had no alarm and nobody was around. The horn had malfunctioned in the middle of the night!

I rushed to the car, popped the hood, and peered at the engine. But what do you do when you are mechanically challenged and the horn is jammed? I considered removing the battery, but that would've taken minutes and our entire block would've been awake by then. So I started the car and prepared to drive away. If I woke up a neighborhood, at least it would be someone else's! As I pulled out of the driveway, the horn stopped.

Silence. My heart thumped in my ears. Slowly, ever so tenderly, I stepped from the car, held my breath, and tiptoed into the house. Since that night, the horn in our Grand Am has not been quite right. Occasionally it honks while I'm driving down the road. So I wave and smile, thankful it is only a few intermittent honks and not a continual one. This method works well, as people in the other vehicles wave and smile, wondering who I am but feeling sure they should know.

Have you ever been awakened from a dreamworld? Have you ever received a wake-up call from God through a circumstance or situation that causes you to take inventory of your life?

I have. Sometimes the sound has been deafening, like a jammed horn. Other times it has been a still, small voice. But each time, God called me to wake up and evaluate my life. He challenged me to rise above mediocrity, to reflect on my faith and experience his best. He placed a passion in my heart to live beyond the mundane, the meager, the halfway, and the insignificant.

If you listen, you will hear God's wake-up call as well. He's calling you to experience more of who he is, to delve deeper into the spiritual life, to take some risks, to surrender. He's calling you to live extraordinarily by faith.

Webster defines "extraordinary" as "going beyond what is usual, regular, or customary." Extraordinary lives are not necessarily filled with hype, popularity, wealth, or fame. They may not be featured on the *Today* show or the nightly news. But they are lived beyond the usual, because they persist in simple faith before God. "Extraordinary" also means "employed for or sent on a special function or service." By listening to God's wake-up call and renewing their faith, people with extraordinary lives reconnect with God's purpose. They serve as "Christ's ambassadors, as though God were making his appeal through [them]" (2 Cor. 5:20).

One way to grow in faith is to look at examples of people of faith who have gone before us. And one way to do that is to look at the eleventh chapter of Hebrews, which chronicles the faith of some of the most famous men and women of the Bible. The Book of Hebrews was a letter written to ordinary people, like you and me, who needed a word from God. Most of them were probably converted Jews, perhaps serving together in a house church in Rome. And they lived during a time when it was becoming increasingly dangerous to admit to being a Christian; in fact, this could seal their death warrants. The rumors kept pouring in, rumors of arrests, of interrogations, of deaths. Rumors of some Christians fleeing to the catacombs and others denying the faith. So Hebrews was written to remind the Christians of Jesus' superiority over every rival and to encourage them to remain unwavering in their faith.

Throughout Hebrews 11 we see how God used everyday people with everyday faith to live extraordinary lives. In fact, this chapter is known as the faith chapter or the "hall of faith." And in it, we see that the life of faith is anything but boring! Along with great victories, the life of faith is full of difficulties, detours, and doubts.

In the following pages, we'll examine people like Abel, Enoch, Noah, Abraham, Moses, and Rahab. We'll learn from contemporary stories of everyday people who experienced God's power by faith. And we will engage in what futurist Faith Popcorn calls "anchoring." Popcorn describes anchoring as a "spiritual exploration in which we ground ourselves by looking back at the past—to prepare for the millennium and beyond."[2] Looking to the past, we find strength to move forward in the future.

As we explore the life of faith, we may hear the deafening sound of God's wake-up call, like a jammed horn, challenging us to open our eyes. Or we may hear the still, small voice of his Spirit prompting us to take inventory of our lives and keep growing. Either way, we will find the life of faith to be anything but predictable and ho-hum.

If we want to live life on the edge, if we want to discover the power of God moving in our lives, if we want a renewed passion for God, we must submit to him and learn from those who have walked in faith before us. Though we can't go back and change the past, we can experience the adventure God has for us today. We can live extraordinarily, like those in Hebrews 11, through faith's transforming power.

ONE

# A FAITH THAT RIDES TIDES

*Lord, help me to do great things as though they were little, since I do them in your power; and little things as though they were great, since I do them in your name.*[1]

BLAISE PASCAL

When Italian forces retreated from North Africa during World War II, they left the harbor unusable by sinking huge concrete barges into the sandbar across the entrance. The Allies desperately needed the harbor, but they could not budge the concrete barges. So they devised a brilliant plan. They filled gigantic oil tanks with enough water to be heavy, yet light enough to float. Then they chained the tanks to the barges below the water. The tide lifted the tanks, which raised the barges from the sandbar below. Once free, the barges moved easily.[2] The Allies used the tides to harness incredible force.

"Tide" is a generic word used to describe the ebb and flow of the sea levels in relation to land. Shakespeare used the image of the ocean tides to speak of opportunities that can bring great achievement or, when missed, great failure. He wrote,

> There is a tide in the affairs of men
> Which, taken at the flood, leads on to fortune;
> Omitted, all the voyage of their life
> Is bound in shallows and in miseries.
> On such a full sea are we now afloat;
> And we must take the current when it serves,
> Or lose our ventures.[3]

This passage points to the incredible power of the tides but also notes that they are irretrievable and unstoppable. The tides' power comes at distinct moments of time. If we miss the flood, we are left in shallows and miseries, having lost our ventures.

Being carried by the tides provides a moving picture for the life of faith. Each day we face choices that allow us to be a part of God's plan. If we live in faith and allow God in the details of our lives, we experience the power of tide riding. We partner with God and witness him do amazing things. If we do not catch the tide, we miss the blessing God has for us.

If we ignore God's word and warnings, we remain near the shore—stuck in the sandbar. I have been stuck in the sandbar of shame and guilt, unwilling to accept God's forgiveness. I've wallowed in addiction and pain, refusing God's healing. I've wrestled with meaninglessness, blind to God's meaning. By choice I remained stuck. I could have viewed my situation differently, lived in faith, and ridden the tides. I could have experienced freedom.

What is your sandbar? Perhaps your marriage is empty, and you wonder how to continue. Maybe depression grips you, and you long to wake up with a desire to live. Doubt may paralyze you with questions for which you have no answers. Job anxiety may render you fruitless. Whatever your sandbar, chain yourself to God through faith and allow the Spirit's tide to lift and move you. Do what the Allies did— ride the tides!

Faith will not make your problems vanish, but it will empower you to tap into resources beyond your own. Addiction may haunt, but God's power can bring victory. Depression may cast shadows, but faith's light can pierce clouds. One woman struggling with severe depression wrote, "I'm beginning to see faith as the flip side of depression. It, too, colors everything. I cannot always explain it to others, and yet gradually it is bringing light into my dark life."[4] God brings change through faith.

## What Is Faith?

If transforming faith leads to an extraordinary life, what exactly is faith? When I was growing up, my mom would wake me up in the morning by singing at the top of her lungs "Oh, What A Beautiful Mornin'" from *Oklahoma!* When she got to the line "everything's going my way," she would drag out the word "way" as she opened the miniblinds to the blinding light. Talk about trauma! I was forced to be a morning person. The quicker I rose, the quicker she would stop singing. For some, faith is like that line from *Oklahoma!* It's only a feeling that everything's going their way.

A schoolboy once defined faith as something you believe when you know it is not true. T. H. Huxley said, "Faith is the one unpardonable sin."[5] David Hume claimed faith is a solid feeling. Ambrose Pierce, in his *Devil's Dictionary,* described faith as "belief without evidence in what is told by one who speaks without knowledge of things without parallel."[6]

The Bible paints another picture. Hebrews reads, "Now faith is being sure of what we hope for and certain of what we do not see" (Heb. 11:1). This is a description of faith, not a definition. Faith means belief, trust, confidence. Faith involves being sure and certain of things unseen. The Greek word translated "being sure" in Hebrews 11:1 is translated as "exact representation" in Hebrews 1:3. There it refers to Jesus. As Jesus is the exact representation of God, faith is the exact representation of things unseen.

In our visual age, we say, "I'd have to see it to believe it." But in God's eyes, faith is belief in the unseen. Seeing from his perspective transforms. Matthew Henry said, "Faith demonstrates to the eye of the mind the reality of these things which cannot be discerned by the eye of the body."[7]

I remember the day I started wearing glasses. For some time, my eyes had grown weaker, but I had put off going to the optometrist. Then clocks became increasingly blurry. Freeway exit signs got closer before I could decipher them. Eventually, I cut vehicles off while exiting the freeway. So I finally visited the optometrist. When I put on my new glasses, the world came alive. The blurs became sharp and focused. Trees seemed incredibly green and leaves became three-dimensional. Highway signs were large enough to read!

This illustrates faith's way of seeing. Before I reached out to God, my life appeared colorless and blurry. I had become a very angry person, angry at everything and everybody. So I turned to drugs, first just at parties, but soon on a regular basis. It was my way of coping with the meaninglessness and emptiness I felt inside. My family tried to reach out to me, and my true friends attempted to help. But I was like a ghost. It was the eighties, and the motto of my life was captured in *Bill and Ted's Excellent Adventure*: "Party on, dude."

Eventually, I became sick of the party. I entered my bedroom and shut the door at the age of seventeen. I felt so tired—tired of the lies, the drugs, the betrayed relationships, the emptiness, and the guilt. I felt tired of being tired. So I fell to my knees and surrendered to God.

He could have replied, "Jud, you've destroyed everything I put into your life. I gave you a wonderful family whom you worried to death. I blessed you with great relationships, which you severed. I gave you friends, most of whom you betrayed or cheated. I gave you a healthy body, which you tried to destroy. You lashed out at everything I put into your path with a self-inflicting rage that came from nowhere." Instead, he said something I did not expect: "Welcome home." Two simple words, not spoken audibly, but impressed on my heart and filled with unimaginable grace and love that changed my life. I began to participate in the world's greatest drama—the kingdom of God. The sheer thrill and joy of living by faith became part of my daily life.

Faith's way of seeing transformed me. It reduced my mountains to molehills, calmed raging storms, brought peace to chaos and hope in difficulty. The mundane details of life took on significance.

Don't miss the color and clarity of life. Place your faith in Jesus Christ, put on spiritual glasses, and *see* differently. Allow his purpose to give significance to your life.

## Faith Is a Verb

Faith is not only a way of seeing but a way of living. Kathleen Norris recorded her twenty-year journey to faith in *Amazing Grace: A Vocabulary of Faith*. In it she writes:

> No small part of my religious conversion has been coming to know that faith is best thought of as a verb, not a "thing" that you either have or you don't. Faith is not discussed as an abstraction in the gospels. Jesus does not talk about it so much as respond to it in other people, for example, saying to a woman who has sought him for a healing, "thy faith hath made thee whole."[8]

In a sense, faith is a verb, a lifestyle. Faith and action walk side by side. Hit the street and ask people if they believe in God, and you will hear thousands of affirmatives. But for many, those beliefs have no application in life.

Faith, however, is more than lip service. If everything I own is God's, my generosity should reflect that. If God's love changed my life, it should be obvious. James writes:

> What good is it, my brothers, if a man claims to have faith but has no deeds? Can such faith save him? Suppose a brother or sister is without clothes and daily food. If one of you says to him, "Go, I wish you well; keep warm and well fed," but does nothing about his physical needs, what

good is it? In the same way, faith by itself, if it is not accompanied by action, is dead.

JAMES 2:14–17

The hard questions are: Do my beliefs and actions resemble each other? Do people know me by my love?

Looking at the people in Hebrews 11, I find hope and challenge. Here was Cain, who was the first hypocrite and murderer. And Noah, a warrior of faith, who passed out, drunk and naked, in his tent after the flood. Abraham obeyed God's call, but not completely; he was supposed to leave his father's household and family, but he brought his father with him. Moses, a murderer, roamed the desert for forty years, struggling with failure and destiny. Rahab was a prostitute who became a hero through an act of faith. God desires a verblike faith, but faith is still filled with human folly, as we see in these biblical examples. But in these examples we also see that grace seasons the journey from beginning to end.

## Eveline's Verblike Faith

Eveline Rivers's faith is a verb. Her life is extraordinary. If Rivers wrote a book, she would title it, *God, I Think You Picked the Wrong Person*. But after time with her, I'm convinced God knew what he was doing.

Rivers directs the Eveline Rivers Christmas Project, which helps families meet their clothing, hygiene, and personal needs. Compassion is her gift. She takes John's command seriously: "Let us not love with words or tongue but with actions and in truth" (1 John 3:18).

The project began in 1979 when Eveline felt moved to help one family at Christmas. She contacted an elementary school principal, who recommended a family of eleven children whose mother had passed away due to a brain tumor. The father seemed reluctant to accept help, but he eventually consented.

Eveline rounded up friends and family to provide for the children. They bought snow boots, coats, clothes, and toys. After learning that the kids slept three to a twin bed and four to a double, one of Eveline's friends built six bunk beds so that each child had a bed. A church paid for the sheets and pillowcases.

Then the group discovered that the ten-year-old child filled a red wagon with laundry and hauled it to the laundromat daily. So another church group provided a washer and dryer. People from all over Eveline's community helped.

Eveline's principal friend pointed her to other families. At first she didn't want to burden herself with more work, but after seeing the needs of the families, she felt called to act. That Christmas she helped forty-three children. Dozens of ordinary acts of faith led to life-changing results in these families.

As Eveline and friends lived their faith, the ministry grew. Many times Eveline walked by faith, not sight. For instance, at one point the project moved into six small trailers and desperately needed a permanent home. Eveline struggled through this valley; she had no idea how to move forward. She and her husband, Wayne, prayed and drove all over town, searching for a place to relocate. Then, walking into a warehouse, they sensed peace. "It was as though God said, 'Eveline, I built this building thirty years ago, but I knew you would eventually get here. I placed the coat room, the bicycle repair shop, storage, offices and things to take care of all your needs.'"[9] The only problem: They had no money and the warehouse had a market price of $250,000.

So they made contacts, researched, and submitted nine grants for funding. Amazingly, every request was granted, to the exact cost of the building. Again God showed himself faithful. After many gallons of paint and much hard work, the project had a permanent home. By Christmas 2000, after twenty-one years, the Eveline Rivers Christmas Project had grown to care for over seven thousand children yearly. Innumerable needs continue to be met as they fulfill their slogan—"Make a Child Smile."

In 2000 Eveline received the Texas Governor's Award for volunteerism. Even at the ceremony, she moved the spotlight to others, saying, "This is for our community. I could not make this project work without the whole community coming together, using their resources and their time." Thanks to Eveline Rivers's verblike faith, thousands of lives have been touched. She has everyday problems, but God uses her faith to do extraordinary things.

You, too, can live a significant life! Begin today with a verblike faith. Follow Eveline's example and let your beliefs show in your actions.

## Faith's Assurance

Faith's way of seeing and living is not without assurances. Hebrews offers an illustration of our assurance. "By faith we understand that the universe was formed at God's command, so that what is seen was not made out of what was visible" (Heb. 11:3). The amazing spectacle of what is seen testifies to the unseen. The beauty and complexity of creation assures us of our faith's validity.

Faith starts with a belief in the creator God. If we accept the opening verses of the Bible, we can accept the entire Bible. Genesis begins, "In the beginning God created the heavens and the earth" (Gen. 1:1). The first verse teaches that there is a God and that earth had a beginning and was created.

This belief cuts against public-school teaching. From secular teachers we learn that the earth and humanity are products of chance. The beauty and complexity of the universe arose from no rhyme and for no reason. In the beginning there was nothing. Over a googolplex of years, nothing became something, which expanded. And over another googolplex of years this something exploded, forming everything. Nothing formed our seas, skies, and landscapes. Nothing gave the ability to think and love. Who knows or cares where nothing is now? Nothing made nothing something, therefore nothing is no longer nothing, because it is something. Get it?!

Hebrews says we understand our origin by faith. In other words, we have assurance when we see through faith's lenses and realize God created everything by his word.

Once I hiked the Smoky Mountains with friends. We trekked during a period when I was wrestling with some major decisions. I needed clarity. Looking over a vast valley, I saw the sun peering spectacularly through the clouds, casting shadows across the valley. I stood speechless, awed by the beauty of creation.

One friend said, "How can you look at that and say there is no Creator?" In that moment, my faith found assurance. If God's power could create that kind of beauty, his power could meet my needs! Assurance that "what is seen was not made out of what was visible," that God spoke and creation was formed, gave me tremendous hope.

Without knowing how the issues I faced would work out, I trusted God, submitted to the tide of his love, and accepted ambiguity.

Next time doubt paralyzes you, go outside and observe. Creation itself can build your faith. Take lessons from the birds, who do not worry or doubt, but trust. Discover assurance in God's power.

## Catch the Tide

God creates tides around the world. He moves and forms people, and through faith and submission, their lives make a difference. I know people who experience tide riding at its best. Their lives are not perfect or free of pain. Their faith is weak at times, strong at others, but they live extraordinary lives for God.

A dentist surrendered to God's call. "God," he said, "all I have is yours. My time, my money, my business, my clients. Do with it what you will." From that moment, God moved noticeably in his life. Now this man has more time, serves more patients, and experiences more of God. His focus has shifted from the business of the moment to the bigger picture of God's work. And he is in for the ride of his life.

One church's women's ministry asked God for direction in reaching their community. They followed his call to the prisons, and their ministry exploded in weeks. Sharing Hope Ministry serves incarcerated women through correspondence and Bible studies. Receiving over 800 letters a month from female inmates, a team of 175 volunteers mails thousands of Bibles and Bible studies. These women volunteers ride in God's timing, Spirit, and power.

25

A successful businessman felt led to help children in Mexico. Following God's direction, he now sends over 1,500 Christmas gifts a year to needy children. Each gift includes a Spanish Bible and plenty of candy. The joy of sharing God's Word with children in remote areas makes him feel as if his gifts bless him more than they do the children.

A woman who overcame colon cancer uses the experience to share her faith with other cancer survivors. "Who would have thought my cancer would bring someone to Christ?" she asks. God did.

A nurse touches the lives of over four hundred people a month. She has a goal to share her faith with forty of them. Waiting until she senses a nudge from God saying "Now would be a good time," she catches the tide. She is awestruck by the way God uses her to bring faith, encouragement, and light to others.

These people ride tides of faith, even through incredible storms. They are transformed. You can be transformed as well—you can be free from the sandbar of a meaningless existence. Experience life as God meant it to be.

### Put On Faith's Lenses

Getting new glasses or contacts always requires adjustment. Your eyes must learn to see through them. You must also learn to see life through faith's lenses, so that each relationship, moment, and day takes on greater meaning and wonder. Oswald Chambers said, "Faith is the inborn capacity to see God behind everything, the wonder that keeps you an eternal child. Wonder is the very essence of life."[10] Do you see God in everything? Do you have that sense of wonder? Allow faith to change the way you see.

### Act-ivate Your Faith

Alcoholics Anonymous says: "Fake it until you make it." In other words, act out of obedience even when you don't feel like it. Feelings follow actions. Read Hebrews 11 and notice the phrase "by faith" associated with actions or events. Pick one area in your life that needs action and act as if you feel spiritual strength there. Make faith a verb—activate it.

### Lose Sight of Land

In 1577 Sir Francis Drake became one of the first humans to circumnavigate the world. Just before his ship sailed, he prayed this tide-riding prayer:

> Disturb us, O Lord, when
> We are too well pleased with ourselves.
> When our dreams have come true
> Because we dreamed too little,
> When we arrived safely
> Because we sailed too close to the shore. . . .
>
> Disturb us, O Lord, to dare more boldly,
> To venture on wider seas
> Where storms will show Your mastery;
> Where losing sight of land,
> We shall find the stars.
>
> We ask You to push back the horizons of our hopes
> And push us in the future
> In strength, courage, hope, and love.
> This we ask in the name of our Captain,
> Who is Jesus Christ.[11]

In essence, Drake called out to God to fill him and his crew with tide-riding faith. He prayed for the courage to lose sight of land in order to find the stars. By chaining ourselves to God, we can be free from the sandbar that holds us down. We can experience the power of tide riding. We can discover the stars. Submit to God's control and allow him to move in your life. You won't regret it!

# TWO

# A FAITH THAT LEAVES A LEGACY

*What we do in this life echoes in eternity.*

GENERAL MAXIMUS, *GLADIATOR*

Someone once said we should make life's major decisions in a cemetery. Sounds a little morbid, but a cemetery reminds us of ultimate things and helps us plan with the end in mind. When I was growing up, a cemetery separated my best friend's house from mine, and I read epitaphs while walking to his house. Epitaphs speak to our legacy. For example, Martin Luther King Jr.'s epitaph reads in part, "Free at

FAITH THAT GOES THE DISTANCE

last, free at last, thank God Almighty, I'm free at last." What an amazing summation of his quest for freedom.

King struggled greatly in life. He was jailed over twenty times. His home was bombed. Falsely accused and labeled insincere, he was called a communist. He was stabbed, ridiculed, and constantly threatened with death. He wrote many sermons in jail.

As the sun set on April 4, 1968, King sat in room 306 of the Lorraine Motel. He was working on a sermon entitled, "Why America May Go to Hell." Growing hungry, he stepped out onto the balcony. In one unexpected flash, a rifle shot hurled King into the wall. One writer said his arms were "stretched out to his sides as if he were being crucified."[1] Within a few moments, King breathed his last and his legend began to unfold. Even today his message of freedom lives and his faith speaks. His epitaph captures his passion.

Chris Leimer researched tombstone epitaphs around the world. Here are some he discovered:[2]

> Here lies my wife; here let her lie!
> Now she's at rest, and so am I.

> He meant well,
> Tried a little,
> Failed much.

> Beneath this sod,
> this lump of clay,
> lies Arabella Young,
> who, on the 24th of May,
> began to hold her tongue.

> The Defense Rests.

Here lies Less More
two shots from a 44
no less, no more.

Dead people do speak. Hebrews tells us "By faith Abel offered God a better sacrifice than Cain did. By faith he was commended as a righteous man, when God spoke well of his offerings. And *by faith he still speaks, even though he is dead"* (Heb. 11:4, emphasis added). Abel's legacy speaks to generation after generation. The message of his life impacts people.

Everyone leaves a legacy, but we easily forget this amidst the business of life. We live day to day without regard for legacy or influence, but our relationship with God paves the way for others to experience faith. The question isn't, "Will I leave a legacy?" but "What kind of legacy will I leave?"

And it's also important to realize that none of us come from a perfect legacy. The good news is that by God's grace we are not bound to repeat the negatives in our legacy. Some people come from a background of alcoholism and addiction. Others have a chain of child abuse in their family. No matter what your legacy is, you can break the chain and create a legacy of faithfulness for future generations.

## Breaking the Chain

Pastor Thomas Dowling received a difficult legacy passed down from previous generations.[3] His grandfather on his father's side was a good man and a committed Christian. But Tom's grandmother, Fannie, inherited a family history of mental illness that profoundly affected his father, Buddy.

31

Buddy was born into mental illness. Fannie committed emotional incest with him in multiple ways. Treated like a girl when he was a child, he was not allowed to cut his hair. He struggled with manic depression and a deeply confusing childhood.

When Tom was born, Buddy loved and encouraged him, but there was a dark side to the legacy. Tom remembers little about his father in childhood—he blocks him out because of abuse. When Tom was very young, the emotional and physical scarring began. The sexual abuse began at age five, after his oldest sister moved out, and continued until he was thirteen. He remembers sleeping protectively, so that his father would not enter his bedroom and touch him.

Tom's mother was a good person trying her best to be mother and father. She knew nothing of the abuse, but Tom showed signs—at age nine, he suffered from eczema, a skin rash due to stress; at twelve, hemorrhoids; at thirteen, he sucked his thumb. These were signals that things were not right at home.

Tom said to me: "The last thing I remember about my abuse is my father standing over me in my bedroom. I am kicking him and telling him to get out of my bedroom and never come back. From that time on he did not mess with me. But he put me on a path which led to a lot of pain. What my dad passed down to me as a little boy was a sexual boundary that was blurred."[4] Attempting to protect Tom, Buddy withdrew emotionally and encouraged Tom from afar rather than sustaining a close relationship.

Tom was confused about the spiritual legacy his father passed on to him. The legacy was one of churchgoing, not faithfulness. They attended church on Sunday morning,

Sunday night, and Wednesday night. His dad served as a deacon, but stepped down due to lack of emotional strength. Tom states, "I am grateful for my church background, but I was confused because my father was two different people. There was the churchgoing man and there was the abusive father."[5] As Tom became a man, his father communicated sorrow and guilt in unspoken ways, hinting about things for which he could never forgive himself.

When Tom married his wife, Susan, he shared his past. "The best thing I ever did was marry my wife," he says. With the help of God and Susan, he chose to break the chain of abuse. He began a career teaching elementary and middle school students in an effort to protect kids. When his own children were born, he made sure they had a positive childhood. He claims: "Instead of passing on the confusing legacy of my father, which was mental illness, abuse, and withdrawal, I decided to do the exact opposite. I wanted my kids to know me. I wanted them to remember me, and I wanted to take an active role in their life. I wanted them to have a well-rounded education. I wanted them to understand that sexuality was a gift from God designed for a marriage relationship. I never wanted them to go through what I went through, or struggle as I had."[6]

Breaking the chain was difficult. Tom struggled with a short fuse like his father's and wrestled with emotional highs and lows. But through it all he sheltered his children from his legacy's dark side.

In 1994 Tom's father passed away. Tom walked around a nearby park and sang, "Oh God, you are my God, and I will ever praise you . . . And step by step you lead me, and I will follow you all of my days."

Tom told me: "I sang that song over and over again. At that point, I totally separated my dad from God. So many men who have dysfunctional dads compare their dads to God. That is why they have trouble trusting, submitting, and identifying with God. At that point I severed that connection finally, and in a new way I understood that God was different than my dad."[7]

Tom began an earnest journey to discover greater health in the aftermath of an unhealthy childhood. He sought sound Christian counseling and fought hard to understand and heal. Today he is not the split person he could be due to his legacy. He is not one person at home and another at church. He is a complete person, finally comfortable with himself. "It is so nice after over thirty-seven years of hating myself to say, 'I like me,'" he said to me with a smile. "If I can pass anything on to my children, it is the ability for them to love themselves as people made in God's image."

Changing the dark side of his legacy was only accomplished by God's grace. Tom said: "With God, every day is a new day. We can start fresh each day. The real essence of a godly man is the fruit of the spirit—love, joy, peace, patience, kindness, goodness, faithfulness, gentleness, self-control. God gives us the ability to live that way, but we have to make the choice. Do we grab onto the legacy of dysfunction, or do we grab onto the legacy of the Lord? Life is a choice, and you can break the chain. You have to be willing to fight hard for health, knowing God is the great physician. You have to understand your past, and then you have to move on from it."[8] Tom's legacy is now one of love, joy, and the courage to break chains of abuse.

We also can leave a positive legacy. Extraordinary lives are lived with an awareness of what is ultimate and they pass on enduring legacies. Abel's life gives insight into a lasting spiritual legacy.

## Authentic Worship

We meet Abel in chapter four of Genesis. He and his older brother, Cain, were the first children of Adam and Eve. They were not born in the Garden of Eden, but walked on an unpolluted and unpopulated earth.

Genesis says Abel "kept flocks" and Cain "worked the soil" (Gen. 4:2). One worked as a shepherd and the other as a farmer.

> In the course of time Cain brought some of the fruits of the soil as an offering to the Lord. But Abel brought fat portions from some of the firstborn of his flock. The Lord looked with favor on Abel and his offering, but on Cain and his offering he did not look with favor.
>
> Genesis 4:3–5

Apparently, God gave instructions on worship prior to this. Though he accepted Abel's worship, he rejected Cain's.

Abel brought fat portions from his flock's firstborn. In the Old Testament, the fat around the kidneys was burnt as an offering. This fat was the choice part of the animal. In offering it, people showed that their loyalty belonged to God; they acknowledged God's ownership of the whole flock and all it produced. Abel's worship was offered with pure motives and a thankful heart.

Cain brought some fruits. The text doesn't say more, except that his offering displeased God. The issue between Cain and Abel's worship may be between plant and animal offerings, but the underlying issue relates to the heart.

35

The difference is between a thoughtless and thoughtful offering, between inauthentic and authentic worship.[9] Cain worshiped inauthentically. But before we judge him, we should remember how easily we get sidetracked in worship, how easily the riptides of the world, the flesh, and the devil distract and carry us away.

A riptide is a current of water that opposes another current. A riptide sucks your legs out from under you and pulls you beneath the water and out to sea. A riptide is deadly.

We live between two opposing forces—God and sin. Submitting to the former leads to extraordinary lives, but submitting to the latter will destroy us like massive riptides. Let's look at some potential riptides that cause havoc in our lives.

## Riptide #1: Traditionalism

Cain's worship displeased God. Some words translated "worship" in Hebrew and Greek mean "bow down." They carry the idea of bowing one's will before God, bowing physically and lifting one's arms in prayer. "Worship" also means sharing in prayer and songs of adoration. Worship gives glory to God in every area of life. We are created to worship.

True worship is confused by traditionalism. Jaroslav Pelikan said, "Tradition is the living faith of the dead; traditionalism is the dead faith of the living."[10] The difference between tradition and traditionalism has nothing to do with traditional hymns or contemporary praise songs. Authentic worship clings to tradition with a vibrant faith anchored in the past, while moving forward on faith's high seas. Traditionalism is dangerous; this is when our habits and customs block what God wants to do in our lives, when authentic worship is reduced to going through motions.

Perhaps Cain struggled in traditionalism's riptide. Maybe he worshiped to fulfill others' expectations. Maybe he brought offerings so he could get on with his day. Maybe his faith, once vibrant and alive, became an afterthought. His sacrifice exhibited, in Pelikan's words, the "dead faith of the living."

Traditionalism easily traps. We view the time we attend church as the only time we need to worship. But even those times can be sucked under the riptide of the familiar. For instance, Sunday morning we arise with the alarm, rub sleepy eyes, and pull ourselves together. A few arguments with the kids and a couple breakfast spills later, we arrive at church. We search out a parking place and find our familiar seat, but are we prepared to worship God authentically?

For years I attended church without understanding worship. My mom recalls that my snoring once interrupted a sermon. Needless to say, I quickly received the elbow and "the look." Church seemed to me like a little girl's comment to a friend as they entered "big church." "Shh," she said, "you have to be quiet because there are people sleeping in here."

One of my first preaching responsibilities was at a retirement home in a rough area of Chicago. I spoke to ten people on average. Most times, several of the residents were asleep by the time I stood to speak. One occasionally snored. I once watched a guy fall asleep and bounce his head off the pew in front of him. Of course, at the end of the service, the residents were quick to say, "Great message. You touched my life!"

Worship involves more than church attendance, no matter if we are awake or not. Worship concerns our entire lives. Authentic worshipers live each day, each moment, in submission to God. When I cued into this, church came alive. I looked forward to church, received strength from it, and worshiped during it.

How do I know when traditionalism's riptide threatens? It's when

I reduce worship to something which only happens at church.

I'm more concerned about something fitting my "church expectations" than if it's biblical.

God must fit my mold of what worship should be like.

Worship is a frustrating interruption to my busy day.

None of these signs mean faith is dead, but they are danger signals pointing to my heart's state. They reveal a shift from vibrant worship directed toward God to self-centered worship focused on my own feelings.

A. W. Tozer called worship the "missing jewel" of the church.[11] Only by remembering how awesome God is can we dig below traditionalism's surface and discover this jewel. God's power should astound us with amazement; his holiness should fill us with awe. He is truly the King of kings.

Consider the Israelites' encounter with God in Exodus.

On the morning of the third day there was thunder and lightning, with a thick cloud over the mountain, and a very loud trumpet blast. Everyone in the camp trembled. Then Moses led the people out of the camp to meet with God, and they stood at the foot of the mountain. Mount Sinai was covered with smoke, because the LORD descended on it in fire. The smoke billowed up from it like smoke from a furnace, the whole mountain trembled violently, and the sound of the trumpet grew louder and louder. Then Moses spoke and the voice of God answered him.

EXODUS 19:16–19

Imagine the people saying at that moment

"I don't like this worship style. I'm not even sure it's biblical."

"All this thunder and lightning. All this pomp and circumstance. Where is the quiet? Where is the reverence?"

"Would you look at Jehudijah's toga? To think she wore that to the mountain, of all places!"

"I'm not getting anything out of this. I'm going back to camp to cook manna."

But they did not concern themselves with the trivial. Enraptured by the greatness of God, they were overwhelmed with awe, wonder, and even fear. The text says, "When the people saw the thunder and lightning and heard the trumpet and saw the mountain in smoke, they trembled with fear" (Exod. 20:18).

They were shaken by God's glory, majesty, and power. Nothing revives faith more quickly than a fresh glimpse of God. People say, "The church just cannot compete with Hollywood." But Hollywood cannot compete with the holy.[12] God is so awesome that no one, no thing, no media form comes close to his glory.

> "To whom will you compare me?
> Or who is my equal?" says the Holy One.
> Lift your eyes and look to the heavens:

Who created all these?
He who brings out the starry host one by one,
    and calls them each by name.
Because of his great power and mighty strength,
    not one of them is missing.

ISAIAH 40:25–26

When traditionalism's riptide threatens, catch a fresh glimpse of God's power and majesty. He is the maker of heaven and earth, and he requires a living faith and vibrant heart. When you prepare for times of worship, such as a church service, remind yourself of God's greatness. Focus on him, not on your feelings or struggles. Exchange the "entertain me" approach to worship for the "exalt him" approach. Worship authentically as Abel did and leave a legacy of faith.

## Riptide #2: Playing the "Religious Card"

Perhaps Cain attempted to look good in front of his brother. By playing the "religious card," he would appear acceptable. (One plays the religious card by acting in a religious way to mislead or manipulate.) After all, he needed to keep up his image.

Years ago, a magazine featured actress Michelle Pfeiffer on the cover. The caption read, "What Michelle Pfeiffer Needs Is . . . Absolutely Nothing!" Later it was discovered that she needed something—over $1,500 of work to clean up the cover photo. Here is a partial listing from the touch-up artist's bill:

Clean up complexion, soften eye lines, soften smile line, add color to lips, trim chin, remove neck lines, soften line under

40

earlobe, add highlights to earrings, add blush to cheek, clean up neckline, remove stray hair, remove hair strands on dress, adjust color and add hair on top of head, add dress on side to create better line, add forehead, add dress on shoulder, soften neck muscle a bit, clean up and smooth dress folds under arm, and create one seam on image on right side.

Total cost of fixing this "perfect" picture: $1,525. Even I could be beautiful for $1,525! Outward appearances can deceive, as in the case of the magazine's cover and in the case of Cain.

Plenty of people manage their image today. They go to church for appearance's sake. With Bibles under their arms, they smile for onlookers. They play the religious card to impress. But internally, there is nothing.

I was once asked to stop being so honest when speaking publicly. After all, this person said, people put you on a pedestal, and you should play the part. But that is precisely the problem the church has faced for years—too many people playing the game!

We must decide if we will impress people or have an impact on them. We impress by upholding an image and playing the game. We have an impact when we let people see us as we are—warts and all. When people see us walk with God, struggle with sin, and deal with daily issues, this may not seem as impressive, but it impacts. If we merely play the religious card, we forfeit the ability to worship authentically and have real impact.

## Riptide #3: Envy

Another riptide involves our relationships with others. When envy develops, we are swept from true worship.

Envy desires first place by bringing others down, and often envy expresses itself in anger and hatred. When Cain saw the acceptance of Abel's sacrifice, he became "very angry, and his face was downcast" (Gen. 4:5). God confronted Cain and said, "Why are you angry? Why is your face downcast?" (Gen. 4:6).

Cain's body language reveals volumes. Envy had devoured him. He was angrier at Abel's acceptance than his own rejection.

Envy occurs all around. In society, we encourage envy and work hard to be envied. Someone quipped, "Envy is not just saying, 'I want my grass greener than yours!' Envy prays your grass turns brown!" Envy is Erma Bombeck jokingly praying, "Lord, if you can't make me thin, then make my friends look fat." And envy happens everywhere: home, school, work, church. Students envy grades, looks, popularity, athletic ability, money, and so on. Envy can consume us like it did Cain.

But the real issue with Cain goes beyond envy. Abel was a righteous man; Cain was not. Cain's sacrifice, his worship, was rejected because of his lifestyle. John writes, "Do not be like Cain, who belonged to the evil one and murdered his brother. And why did he murder him? Because his own actions were evil and his brother's were righteous" (1 John 3:12). Hebrews reads, "By faith [Abel] was commended as a righteous man, when God spoke well of his offerings" (Heb. 11:4).

The Lord approached Cain. "If you do what is right, will you not be accepted? But if you do not do what is right, sin is crouching at your door; it desires to have you, but you must master it" (Gen. 4:6–7). Notice the Lord says, "If you do what is right, will you not be accepted?" If Cain's faith guides him in obedience, he will be accepted. God is fair; he does not play favorites. Cain faced a choice between right and wrong—he could ride the tide of God's power or be lost in envy.

Cain determined to stay angry. Genesis says, "Now Cain said to his brother Abel, 'Let's go out to the field.' And while they were in the field, Cain attacked his brother Abel and killed him" (Gen. 4:8). We witness history's first murder.

Remember the evil queen in Snow White? "Mirror, mirror on the wall, who is the fairest of them all?" she asked.

"Famed is thy beauty, Majesty," the mirror replied. "Behold, a lovely maid I see. Rags cannot hide her gentle grace. Alas, she is more fair than thee." The queen could not live knowing another appeared fairer. Her envy, like Cain's, boiled into murderous rage.

Don't underestimate envy's power; envy subtly strangles the heart. "A heart at peace gives life to the body," Proverbs says, "but envy rots the bones" (Prov. 14:30). Envy harms you more than those you envy.

Envy and anger, like all sin, are riptides desiring to destroy, crouching at the door of our lives. But God promises "No temptation has seized you except what is common to man. And God is faithful; he will not let you be tempted beyond what you can bear" (1 Cor. 10:13). He provides escape routes to overcome temptations. He wanted to deliver Cain, but Cain refused and gratified his envy. He allowed the riptide of inauthentic worship, hypocrisy, envy, and anger to carry him away.

So how do we overcome envy? First, we must refuse to play the comparison game. Comparing leads to frustration. There is always someone more talented, better looking, or more wealthy. In a commencement speech, multibillionaire Ted Turner said:

It's all relative. . . . I sit down and say, I've only got $10 billion, but Bill Gates has $100 billion; I feel like I'm a complete failure in life. So billions won't make you happy if you're worried about someone who's got more than you. . . . So don't let yourself get caught in a trap of measuring your success by how much material success you have.[13]

Second, we should focus on what we have, not on what we don't. Matthew Henry, the famous Bible scholar, was once robbed of his purse. He wrote in his diary: "Let me be thankful. First, I was never robbed before. Second, although they took my purse, they didn't take my life. Third, although they took my all, it was not much. Fourth, let me be thankful because it was I who was robbed and not I who did the robbing." What a perspective!

If you struggle with envy, there is hope. By faith you can experience victory, live righteously, and leave a legacy of faith. God offers you a choice, just as he did Cain. He does not cast you away! Reach out and take his hand. Surrender your pride and submit. Ask God's Spirit to control your life and fill you with power.

## A Legacy of Faith

What did Abel receive for living extraordinarily? Martyrdom! Abel's death confounds the "faith equals success" teaching proclaimed by some televangelists. Faith's life is not necessarily one of comfort, ease, health, and wealth, but it is one lived before God. Abel achieved a testimony, a legacy that speaks after his death.

Abel's faith speaks to God. When Cain was confronted, God said:

44

"Where is your brother Abel?"

"I don't know," he replied. "Am I my brother's keeper?"

The LORD said, "What have you done? Listen! Your brother's blood cries out to me from the ground. Now you are under a curse and driven from the ground, which opened its mouth to receive your brother's blood from your hand. When you work the ground, it will no longer yield its crops for you. You will be a restless wanderer on the earth."

GENESIS 4:9–12

Abel's blood cries for justice.

Hebrews directs us to Abel's entire life, not just his death. Abel lived a life committed to God. This is the greatest legacy one can pass to others. More than riches, fame, power, or influence, our friends and neighbors need to see God's way modeled. Children need the love and discipline that mirrors God's treatment of us. Someone said, "What is important is not what you leave *to* your kids, but what you leave *in* them."

You teach your friends and family many things, but the most important thing is caught as much as taught—a relationship with God. Every other relationship pales in comparison.

## Leaving a Legacy

By faith you can break chains and leave a faithful legacy. Your life can be a light for your family, friends, and future generations. But how?

*Begin with the end in mind.* A visualization recently popularized by Stephen Covey goes like this:

45

Imagine going to the funeral of a loved one. Picture your-self driving to the funeral parlor or chapel, parking the car, and getting out. As you walk inside the building, you notice the flowers, the soft organ music. You see the faces of friends and family you pass along the way. . . . As you walk down the front of the room and look inside the casket, you sud-denly come face to face with yourself. This is your funeral, three years from today. All these people have come to honor you.[14]

You look at the program. Some family members are slated to speak. What will they say about you? A friend will speak next. How will the friend describe your life? Another speaker is from your office. The fourth is from your church. What will they say?

In light of these questions, Covey asks, "What do you want them to say about you?" Answering this question allows you to begin with the end in mind. How do you want to influence those around you? What sort of legacy do you desire to leave? Take a few moments and reflect on what you want those friends and associates to say. Live daily with your legacy in mind.

Ravi Zacharias's ancestors came from the Hindu priest-hood's highest caste. Zacharias converted to Christianity in his late teens and attended college in Canada. Since then, he has lectured all over the world.

Zacharias visited his grandmother's grave in India, thirty years after he surrendered to Christ. She had passed away when he was young. He recalls:

No one had visited her grave for almost thirty years. With his little bucket of water and a small brush, the gardener cleared off the caked-on dirt and, to our utter surprise, under her name, a verse gradually appeared. My wife clasped my hand and said, "Look at the verse!" It read, "Because I live, you shall live also."[15]

The legacy of the grandmother's faith lived and breathed in the grandson standing before her tombstone! Dead people do speak. "Because I live, you shall live also." What message will you leave behind?

Maybe it's time for a walk in a cemetery.

# THREE

# A FAITH THAT WALKS WITH GOD

*Above all, do not lose your desire to walk: every day I walk myself into a state of well-being and walk away from every illness. . . . If one just keeps walking, everything will be alright.[1]*

SØREN KIERKEGAARD

After watching the first man walk on the moon, Dave Kunst decided to do something never done before. On June 20, 1970, Dave and his brother John set out from Waseca, Minnesota, with a mule named Willie Makeit. Their goal: to be the first humans to verifiably walk the earth's landmass. They walked to New York City and touched the Atlantic. Flying to Lisbon, Portugal, they touched the Atlantic on the other side and continued through Europe. Walking across Asia and India, Dave finally reached the Indian Ocean. From there he went to Perth, walked Australia to the Pacific

Ocean and flew to California. On October 5, 1974, Dave walked back into Waseca, Minnesota, after 4 years, 3 months, and 16 days. He had walked 14,450 miles, crossed 4 continents and 13 countries, and wore out 21 pairs of shoes. He had taken more than 20 million steps.

Dave's journey was not without highs and lows. When he walked through the Desert of Death in Afghanistan, temperatures soared to 128 degrees. A group of Afghans thought Dave and John had money, so the Afghans fired weapons at them. Dave suffered injuries; John died. Dave lay in a hospital room recuperating for 4 months. After recovering, he returned to the place where John had died. There, with the American embassy's help, he continued his journey with his other brother, Pete.

Throughout the trip, Dave retired four mules and two dogs. When one mule died in Australia, there was not another for thousands of miles. Lucky for Dave, a schoolteacher named Jenni Samuel drove by and, after striking up a conversation with him, towed his cart for one thousand miles. Dave later married Jenni, and they remain together to this day. His walk earned him the name "Earthwalker" and a listing in the *Guinness Book of World Records*.[2]

If Dave Kunst is the "Earthwalker," Enoch is the "Faithwalker." Enoch walked with God by faith. Tide riders walk with God. Sometimes they walk on water, so to speak, achieving great things by faith. Other times they resemble Peter, who stepped out of the boat and "when he saw the wind, he was afraid and, beginning to sink, cried out, 'Lord, save me!' Immediately Jesus reached out his hand and caught him. 'You of little faith,' he said, 'why did you doubt?'" (Matt. 14:30–31). But either way, these people live extraordinarily by walking in faith.

50

Hebrews includes Enoch in the hall of faith. "By faith Enoch was taken from this life, so that he did not experience death; he could not be found, because God had taken him away. For before he was taken, he was commended as one who pleased God" (Heb. 11:5).

Like Elijah, who rode the chariot to heaven, Enoch did not die. God transported him directly into his presence. And from Enoch's life, we can learn what it means to walk with God in daily acts of faith.

## Enoch the Faithwalker

Enoch lived thousands of years ago at humanity's dawn. Our knowledge of him results from a few verses in Genesis that say:

> When Enoch had lived 65 years, he became the father of Methuselah. And after he became the father of Methuselah, Enoch walked with God 300 years and had other sons and daughters. Altogether, Enoch lived 365 years. Enoch walked with God; then he was no more, because God took him away.
>
> GENESIS 5:21–24

Twice in three verses we read Enoch "walked with God."

Walking with God is a biblical theme. Jacob prayed to the "God before whom my fathers Abraham and Isaac walked" (Gen. 48:15). Jesus said, "Whoever follows me will never walk in darkness, but will have the light of life" (John 8:12). In Genesis, we read God "walked" in the Garden of Eden (Gen. 3:8). "Walked" carries the idea of "pleased" and implies moving with God as he moves with us.

51

My wife, Lori, and I often go for walks. These walks are sacred to us. They denote times to talk and savor our relationship. If we feel disconnected, it is time for a walk.

The same applies to our spiritual lives. When our faith is exhausted, we usually have stopped walking with God, stopped savoring life with God, stopped the spiritual disciplines such as prayer, study, confession, worship, and times of reflection on God's Word. Then it's time for a spiritual walk with God.

As I spend time with God in prayer and reflection, in his Word, in kindness and fellowship, my faith grows vibrant and vital. There is a consistency in my spiritual experience, even in difficulties. But when I allow busyness or laziness to distract, I subtly drift from a dynamic relationship. I may still jump through religious hoops—church, service projects, socials—but I cease to please God by walking in faith.

We need to look to Enoch, who walked in a daily relationship with God. He nurtured his faith, communed with his Maker, and brought joy to God's heart. Make no mistake—Enoch was as busy as we are. He faced pressures, doubts, stress, and temptations. He was human. He lived when righteousness was unpopular and distractions were plentiful.

Jude gives another tidbit of information about Enoch. He writes:

> Enoch, the seventh from Adam, prophesied about these men: "See, the Lord is coming with thousands upon thousands of his holy ones to judge everyone, and to convict all the ungodly of all the ungodly acts they have done in the ungodly way, and of all the harsh words ungodly sinners have spoken against him."
>
> JUDE 14–15

Enoch proclaimed God's message and challenged people to change. He stood for righteousness in a wicked age. Hebrews instructs us to faithwalk as Enoch did. "Without faith it is impossible to please God," reads Hebrews, "because anyone who comes to him must believe that he exists and that he rewards those who earnestly seek him" (Heb. 11:6). Before faith's first stride, we must "believe that [God] exists."

## Faith Believes That God Exists

Enoch lived with a firm belief in God's existence. Extraordinary lives begin with a belief in God. The nineteenth and twentieth centuries challenged God's existence like none other. In 1882 the German thinker Friedrich Nietzsche made his dire statement: "God is dead." But despite Nietzsche's claim, belief in God flourished in the twentieth century. And God is "in" as we advance in the twenty-first century. Everywhere we see interest in spirituality and God. Even the academic community is opening up to God as we witness an explosion of evidence pointing to a creator.

David observed the evidence thousands of years ago. He wrote:

> The heavens declare the glory of God;
> the skies proclaim the work of his hands.
> Day after day they pour forth speech;
> night after night they display knowledge.
> There is no speech or language
> where their voice is not heard.
> Their voice goes out into all the earth,
> their words to the ends of the world.
>
> PSALM 19:1–4

53

Consider our planet's complexity. If earth orbits closer to the sun, we burn up; further away, and we freeze. If the atmosphere thins, we are Kentucky Fried Chicken due to the sun's radiation. The moon orbits 200,000 miles from earth; if it orbits 50,000 miles away, ocean tides would submerge everything twice a day. If the earth's crust thickens 10 feet, we have no oxygen. If the ocean floors deepen a few feet, the carbon dioxide and oxygen balance upsets, destroying all vegetable life. Earth slants at 23 degrees; its tilt produces our seasons. Without its tilt, vapors would move north and south across the earth, creating enormous glaciers and continents of ice. The earth's weight is estimated at six sextillion metric tons. It rotates on its axis at 1,000 miles per hour, 25,000 miles per day, and 9,000,000 miles per year. The earth travels around the sun at 19 miles per second, 1,140 miles per hour, and 600 million miles each year.[3] It does all this smoothly and perfectly, suspended in space by unseen gravitational forces. No wonder Job said, "[God] suspends the earth over nothing" (Job 26:7). Our planet has amazing complexity!

Paul writes, "For since the creation of the world God's invisible qualities—his eternal power and divine nature—have been clearly seen, being understood from what has been made, so that men are without excuse" (Rom. 1:20). Creation witnesses to God's invisible qualities, leaving each person "without excuse."

According to the Bible, the real issue is not lack of evidence, but suppression of evidence due to a wicked heart (Rom. 1:18). David writes, "The fool says in his heart, 'There is no God'" (Ps. 14:1). This does not mean that those who deny God are mentally incapable of intelligent thought. In this case, "fool" carries a moral meaning instead of a mental one. The opposite of the Hebrew "fool" is not "wise," but a term meaning "lovingkindness." The fool is one without lovingkindness, who lives as if there is no covenant between God and humanity. David continues this line of thought: "They are corrupt, their deeds are vile; there is no one who does good" (Ps. 14:1). They suppress the evidence so they can do whatever they choose.

Carl Sagan, the popular scientist, was often fascinated by the many who believed in an unseen God. He once commented to Joan Brown Campbell, "You're so smart, why do you believe in God?"

She responded, "You're so smart, why *don't* you believe in God?" She found his question amazing since he believed in black holes without ever seeing one.

Sagan did not waver in his unbelief. When he died, his wife, Ann Druyan, said, "There was no deathbed conversion. No appeals to God, no hope for an afterlife, no pretending that he and I, who had been inseparable for twenty years, were not saying good-bye forever."

Ann was asked, "Did he want to believe?"

"Carl never wanted to believe," she answered. "He wanted to *know*."[4]

He died without hope, without a future. He and his wife said good-bye forever.

But the life of faith is based on "being sure of what we hope for and certain of what we do not see" (Heb. 11:1). We can't put God in a test tube, but we can walk by faith and experience the joy there. Faithwalkin' starts with a belief that God exists, and according to Hebrews, our first stride is to believe that God rewards those who seek him.

## Walking with God

Statistics reveal that 95 percent of Americans believe in God or a universal force, but only 67 percent believe in a God who is "the all-powerful, all-knowing Creator of the universe who rules the world today."[5] Many who believe in a personal God live like he is uninvolved with human affairs. Their lives lead one to think that God wound the world like a watch and stepped back to let it run its course. They don't involve God in their decision-making process. They may make it to church now and then, but their faith changes nothing. This is not walking with God.

To walk with God as Enoch did, we must know God's characteristics. The New Testament reveals four statements that describe God's person and how people walk with him. By looking at these aspects of God, we can learn how to do some faithwalkin' of our own.

### God Is Spirit; Walk in the Spirit

"God is spirit" (John 4:24). He is unseen, all-present, all-powerful, and accessible by faith. We are commanded to "walk in the Spirit" so that we do not "fulfill the lust of the flesh" (Gal. 5:16 NKJV). Walking in the Spirit is to "walk by faith, not by sight" (2 Cor. 5:7 NKJV). It is to trust God's unseen hand and depend on his strength. It is to lean on the Spirit's power when powerless. It is to rely on the Spirit's leading when lost. Extraordinary lives are not lived in one's own power; they remain dependent on God's Spirit.

Prayer is essential to walking in the Spirit. Our spiritual experience hinges on communion with God, and prayer allows us to tap God's living water. Without consistent prayer, faith dries up.

I've discovered that I pray best when walking. Somehow walking allows me to focus on God and to listen. But the important thing is not *how* I pray, but *that* I pray. How do you pray best?

Brennan Manning writes of praying continually, even amidst the day's business:

> The Spirit of Jesus provides a way for us to live on the surface and out of the depths at the same time. On the surface we can think, dialogue, plan, and be fully present to the demands of daily routine. Simultaneously and deeply within, we can be in prayer, adoration, thanksgiving, and attentiveness to the Spirit. . . . What masters of the interior life recommend is the discipline of "centering down" throughout the day: a quiet, persistent turning to God while driving, cooking, conversing, writing, and so on. After weeks and months of practice, relapses, discouragement, and returns to the center, this discipline becomes a habit. Brother Lawrence called it "the practice of the presence of God."[6]

Through prayer and submission we can bear the fruit of the Spirit.

Don't be overwhelmed by prayer. Start with five concentrated minutes a day. Slip away to a quiet place and pray. Over time, this will grow more comfortable and you won't be able to stop in five minutes. Don't feel like you must pray an hour for it to be legitimate. Start small and allow God to grow in your heart.

### God Is Light; Walk in the Light

When Robert Louis Stevenson was a young boy, his nanny called him to come to bed. Unresponsive to her calling, he stared out the window at lamplighters who lit the old street lamps.

"What in the world are you looking at?" she asked.

"Look, nanny," he said, "those men are poking holes in the darkness."

We are called to poke holes in the darkness by living in God's light. John says, "God is light; in him there is no darkness at all" (1 John 1:5). This means God is absolute righteousness and truth. He is perfect morally (he is holy) and intellectually (he is truth).

John exhorts us to "walk in the light, as [God] is in the light" (1 John 1:7). Walking in the light involves living and thinking according to truth. To live in the truth, we must study and know the truth. This involves reading the Bible along with other books. In study, we allow God's truth to shine light into the center of our being, revealing God's way and revealing us to ourselves. We conform our lives to God's Word and model our behavior on his precepts. We let our lives reflect his truth to the world. We poke holes in the darkness.

### God Is Love; Walk in Love

Love is distorted in our time. Forrest Gump said, "I'm not a smart man, but I know what love is." That makes him one of the smartest men around! Today, love can mean anything: lust, greed, feelings, duty, honor.

Love's meaning is easily lost and distorted in pop culture. Think of the following lyrics:

58

"Hello, I love you, won't you tell me your name."
"Love me tender."
"Fifty ways to leave your lover."
"Can you feel the love tonight?"

But the Greeks understood love's complexity. They used four words to describe love. One of those words, *agape*, is the central word for God's love. *Agape* carries the idea of being generous for the sake of others and the idea of unconditional love. *Agape* means God loves us in spite of ourselves, our past, our mistakes, and our failures. As God says, "I have loved you with an everlasting love; I have drawn you with loving-kindness" (Jer. 31:3).

In view of God's love, we are told to "walk in love, as Christ also has loved us and given Himself for us, an offering and a sacrifice to God for a sweet-smelling aroma" (Eph. 5:2 NKJV). But although love is easy to talk about, it is hard to accomplish. We tend to love each other "because" or "when," rather than "in spite of," as God does. Peter tells us to "love one another deeply, from the heart" (1 Pet. 1:22). "Deeply" means "strained" or "stretched." Some people are hard to love! Loving them is a strain and a stretch. Loving those from the same socioeconomic background who live similar lifestyles is easy. But we are called to love those who are different, difficult, and challenging. We don't get to pick and choose.

Albert Schweitzer once said, "The greatest person alive in the world at this moment is some unknown individual in some obscure place who, at this hour, has gone in love to be with another person in need."[7] Simple acts of love form the substance of extraordinary lives. But we cannot show *agape* through our own power; it is supernatural.

God shows *agape* through us as we walk with him. Our challenge is to submit to God's Spirit and allow God's love to flow through us.

### God Is Holy; Walk in Holiness

Enoch walked with the God who "is holy" (1 Pet. 1:15). God's holiness is his most comprehensive characteristic. In the Bible, we read of the seraphim, angelic beings, singing to one another: "Holy, holy, holy is the LORD Almighty; the whole earth is full of his glory" (Isa. 6:3). Heaven's praise continues day and night: "Holy, holy, holy is the Lord God Almighty, who was, and is, and is to come" (Rev. 4:8).

We often miss the meaning of the triple repetition of "holy." Repitition is a literary technique in the Hebrew language that is used for emphasis.[8] God is not just holy; he is not even holy, holy. He is holy, holy, holy. As R. C. Sproul says, "The Bible never says that God is love, love, love; or mercy, mercy, mercy; or wrath, wrath, wrath; or justice, justice, justice. It does say that he is holy, holy, holy, that the whole earth is full of his glory."[9]

When "holy" is used to describe God, it is a synonym for *all* his attributes. Holiness contains the idea of moral purity, but it extends beyond to encompass God. "Holy" sets him apart as the all-knowing, all-present Creator and sustainer of the cosmos.

And we are commanded to walk in holiness: "But just as he who called you is holy, so be holy in all you do; for it is written: 'Be holy, because I am holy'" (1 Pet. 1:15–16). To be holy is to strive for purity, to be set apart, to live a life that brings God honor and glory.

Before we married, Lori and I agreed I would take out the trash. We generate our share, which inevitably stacks up at the back door. My challenge is getting through our backyard while our St. Bernard practically tackles me. She is convinced that beyond the slim plastic lining of the trash bag is a T-bone steak ready to be devoured.

To be holy is to continually take out the trash from our lives. Maybe our trash is an attitude of unforgiveness, an addiction, an affair, a habit of lying, stealing, or cheating. Maybe it is pride or greed. Let the trash remain inside and it stinks, rots, and attracts bugs and disease. Of course, nobody *wants* to take out the trash. I don't come home, saying giddily, "Oh boy, I get to haul the stinky trash to the dumpster in the hot sun!" But I choose to do it, even though I don't feel like it.

How do we take out the trash in our lives? We confess sin, ask for grace, and prayerfully lean on God's Spirit to bring change. There are always hindrances, of course. Our tendency is to procrastinate until tomorrow. And Satan, like my St. Bernard, does everything in his power to keep the trash inside. He trips us up and convinces us it isn't worth taking out. But despite my dislike of taking out the trash, I sure feel good when it's done. The house smells better, too! Similarly, the freedom and joy that result from taking out our internal trash is amazing.

What sins stink up your life? What do you need to haul to the dumpster? Don't procrastinate and don't believe Satan's lies. Trash attracts corruption and decay. It develops foul odor and repels. Make a trip to the dumpster!

## Walk This Way!

When we walk in God's Spirit, light, love, and holiness, we live lives that make a difference. We take strides of faith

61

that bring God pleasure. Along with Enoch, we discover that God "rewards those who earnestly seek him" (Heb. 11:6). We live in expectancy before God.

Expectancy is key to faith. If we stop walking in expectancy, we wallow in a spiritual rut. So we must pray and live believing God intervenes. "True faith," writes C. S. Lewis, "is never found alone; it is accompanied by expectation."[10] There is nothing more radical, exciting, and fresh than living in expectancy before God. In Jeremiah God says, "You will seek me and find me when you seek me with all your heart" (Jer. 29:13). And Jesus once said, "So I say to you: Ask and it will be given to you; seek and you will find; knock and the door will be opened to you" (Luke 11:9). Ask God to guide and direct. He promises to respond.

God's reward for seeking him is not a blank check—sometimes the last thing we need is more things. Earnestly seeking God means we desire him above all else. The Psalmist says, "Delight yourself in the Lord and he will give you the desires of your heart" (Ps. 37:4). "Delight" in Hebrew literally means "soft and pliable." Soft and pliable in God's hands, we are open to his will and purpose. So the desires of our hearts change.

Earnestly seeking God also involves praying with faith. James tells us to ask God for wisdom, but in asking, we

> must believe and not doubt, because he who doubts is like a wave of the sea, blown and tossed by the wind. That man should not think he will receive anything from the Lord; he is a double-minded man, unstable in all he does.
>
> James 1:6–8

Do you watch and wait in expectancy? Do you realize you pray to the all-knowing, all-present, all-powerful Creator of the universe? He can do anything, anywhere, anytime, in any form or fashion. He owns the cattle on a thousand hills. His hand stretches across the expanse of the universe. His word created all that exists. Heaven is his throne, earth his footstool. Expect him to move in response to your faith.

## Faithwalkin'

How can you faithwalk to an extraordinary life?

### Take Strides with God

Set aside a daily time and place to pray. Start small and build on it. Surrender daily to God's Spirit. Ask for power to overcome temptation. Allow him into the details of your life! Walk according to his qualities.

| Quality | Way to Walk |
| --- | --- |
| Spirit | Prayer |
| Light | Study |
| Love | Sacrifice |
| Holiness | Repentance |

I am amazed at the number of people who stop walking in faith. Most of them don't choose to stray from the path; they subtly drift. They cease doing daily spiritual disciplines, and before they know it, they lose their way.

Søren Kierkegaard wrote to a friend:

But now to something far more important. I see, to my horror, from what you write that you have stopped walking. Above all, this must not be so. . . . I must emphatically

63

request that you go on walking. . . . My view of life is like that of the parson: "Life is a path." That is why I go walking. As long as I am able to go walking, I fear nothing, not even death.[11]

I echo Kierkegaard—you must not stop walking *in faith*. Jesus promises, "To him who overcomes [who keeps walking in faith], I will give the right to eat from the tree of life, which is in the paradise of God" (Rev. 2:7).

### Know Why You Believe

A person who has faith believes God exists, but not blindly. Faith is based on all kinds of evidence. "Always be prepared," writes Peter, "to give an answer to everyone who asks you to give the reason for the hope that you have" (1 Pet. 3:15). Read Paul Little's *Know Why You Believe* or Lee Strobel's *The Case for Christ*. Learn the evidence that supports faith. Trust God to use it in others' lives.

We don't have to walk earth's landmass, like Dave Kunst, and we may never make the *Guinness Book of World Records*. But walking by faith with the earth's Creator records our names in his Book of Life. Just as Enoch was transported to God's presence, we also will see God's face. At that time, the mountains and valleys we have traversed with him will be worth more than the suffering we endured.

Keep faithwalkin'!

# FOUR

# A Faith That Obeys God

*The waters are rising, but so am I. I am not going under, but over.[1]*

CATHERINE BOOTH

Ancient Irish missionaries took to the sea without specific destinations—they put their faith in God to carry them by the wind and tides. Wherever they landed, they shared their faith in Christ. Some were never seen again. They were tide riders in the most literal sense.

Though I do not recommend seafaring without oars and rudders, these missionaries are a powerful image of faith: They lived each day in submission to God and were willing to go and do whatever he desired. A. W. Tozer claimed there are three marks of one who is crucified, or truly submitted to God. First, this person faces only one direction. Second, this person never turns back. And third, this person no longer makes plans on his or her own. This is tide-riding faith. This is Noah's faith.

Noah lived during a difficult time. In Genesis chapter three, Adam and Eve ate from the forbidden tree and were cast out of Eden. From then on, things went in a downward spiral. By chapter six, Noah's time, we read of murder, jealousy, anger, and polygamy. God "saw how great man's wickedness on the earth had become, and that every inclination of the thoughts of his heart was only evil all the time. The LORD was grieved that he made man on the earth, and his heart was filled with pain" (Gen. 6:5–6).

We often perceive God as immovable and unemotional. But he is not so remote that he experiences no emotion; he grieves at our lack of loyalty. Here we discover that "his heart was filled with pain."

Through eyes filled with pain, God looked across the world and concluded, "I will wipe out mankind, whom I have created, from the face of the earth" (Gen. 6:7). He decided to start over. The good news is "Noah found favor in the eyes of the LORD" (Gen. 6:8). He had lived an extraordinary life.

## Remarkable Faith

Hebrews places Noah in faith's hall of fame: "By faith Noah, when warned about things not yet seen, in holy fear built an ark to save his family. By his faith he condemned the world and became heir of the righteousness that comes by faith" (Heb. 11:7).

God commanded Noah to begin shipbuilding because a flood was coming. Noah probably lived in Mesopotamia, between the Tigris and Euphrates rivers, far from any great body of water. The Bible says a stream or mist rose from the earth and watered the surface (Gen. 2:6). Up until that time, Noah may have never experienced rain. So for 120 years he took up his building tools, even though he may have never seen rain! Imagine a more incredible display of faith than Noah cutting down that first tree. He rode faith's tide so that one day he could ride the ocean's tide.

According to the lowest estimates, this boat sat 483 feet long, 73 feet wide, and 44 feet high—almost one and a half football fields long and over four stories tall. The deck covered 96,000 square feet, and the total space of all decks was 1.3 million cubic feet.[2] Quite a ship! John MacArthur writes, "Naval engineers have discovered that the dimensions and shape of the ark form the most stable ship design known."[3]

Noah built that ship in faith and experienced God's best. It wasn't always easy, though. Like Enoch, Noah spread God's message, because he was more than a builder, he was a "preacher of righteousness" (2 Pet. 2:5). His ministry lasted 120 years, the time it took him to build the ark. Can you believe it? Noah preached to the same rebellious people for 120 years! I visualize him preaching from the ship's scaffold during construction, or traveling the countryside warning friends of "what we do not see" (Heb. 11:1).

How many "Noah jokes" did Noah and family endure over 120 years? How much scoffing and how many naysayers? In spite of the circumstances, however, Noah remained faithful. He knew God would relent if the people repented. God had told him:

If at any time I announce that a nation or kingdom is to be uprooted, torn down and destroyed, and if that nation I warned repents of its evil, then I will relent and not inflict on it the disaster I had planned. And if at another time I announce that a nation or kingdom is to be built up and planted, and if it does evil in my sight and does not obey me, then I will reconsider the good I had intended to do for it.

JEREMIAH 18:7–10

So Noah stood alone and shared God's message of hope. But in the end, only he and his family entered the ark. Peter says, "God waited patiently in the days of Noah while the ark was being built. In it only a few people, eight in all, were saved through water" (1 Pet. 3:20). The entire world perished when God's judgment rained down.

## Get in the Ark!

The flood of God's judgment devastated Noah's generation. God promises to judge and destroy again, but not by water. Next time he will destroy the earth by fire.

Speaking of the flood in Noah's day, Peter writes:

By these waters also the world of that time was deluged and destroyed. By the same word the present heavens and earth are reserved for fire, being kept for the day of judgment and destruction of ungodly men.

But do not forget this one thing, dear friends: With the Lord a day is like a thousand years, and a thousand years are like a day. The Lord is not slow in keeping his promise, as some understand slowness. He is patient with you, not wanting anyone to perish, but everyone to come to repentance.

68

But the day of the Lord will come like a thief. The heavens will disappear with a roar; the elements will be destroyed by fire, and the earth and everything in it will be laid bare.

2 PETER 3:6–10

God longs for us to heed his warnings and turn. He longs for us to get in the ark, so to speak, and escape the coming judgment.

Jesus describes the situation when the flood came:

"Just as it was in the days of Noah, so also will it be in the days of the Son of Man. People were eating, drinking, marrying and being given in marriage up to the day Noah entered the ark. Then the flood came and destroyed them all. . . . It will be just like this on the day the Son of Man is revealed."

LUKE 17:26–27, 30

The people lived it up, oblivious to God's commands. Judgment came swiftly and devastatingly.

America has experienced economic abundance, which is a blessing and a curse. We can accomplish so much with our unprecedented wealth, but wealth can also destroy. People speak of being faithful to God in failure and poverty; the real challenge is being faithful in success and prosperity.

We load ourselves down with debt; we eat, drink, and wed, but do we live in faith and reverence? Spiritual renewal comes as we recognize that although things appear to continue apart from God, he still sits on his throne, and we still live before him. Faith obeys God's command and gets in the ark.

69

## Staying Afloat When the Flood Comes

Floods come in the form of judgment, as was the case with Noah, but they also come in our own difficult circumstances. Staying afloat in our postmodern world is a challenge. Storms rage and waves threaten to capsize us. The flood may advance in the form of cancer, divorce, an estranged child, a loved one's death, bankruptcy, or layoff. But whatever form the flood takes, you can stay afloat. "The waters are rising," wrote Catherine Booth, "but so am I. I am not going under, but over."[4]

Take the case of Gil Farren. One day her pager went off and the number of her doctor's office appeared. When she phoned him back, he requested more tests immediately. The pager signaled a flood being unleashed in her life.

It had all begun when she picked up a light piece of furniture in early 1999. Feeling a pain in her side, she assured herself it was no big deal. She had been feeling tired after small tasks, but after all, so much had occurred in her life recently. Her father had passed away in October of the previous year, and the responsibility to settle his estate weighed heavily on her. Her work as a victim assistance coordinator for her county added extra strain. At forty-seven she felt too young and busy to be sick. She thought rest and relaxation would restore her health, but her side continued to hurt, prompting her to visit the doctor.

All the tests came back negative, but the pager that fateful day turned relief into serious concern. More tests revealed 473 tumor markers. The average person has under 35. A biopsy confirmed stage IV breast cancer that had metastasized to the bones.

Gil and her husband, James, were thrust into the world of cancer—one test after another, one opinion after another, one waiting room after another, one doctor after another. James described the experience: "Cancer is like walking to the beach and saying, 'That's the ocean.' At first, it is just the ocean. But before you know it there is a three hundred-foot-high wave coming toward you, threatening to wash you away."[5] The wave was overwhelming and the flood waters were rising. The flood demanded every reservoir of spiritual, physical, and emotional strength to survive.

Gil began chemotherapy in May of 1999, but since the cancer had metastasized to her bones, she took a radical step and underwent a stem-cell transplant. Her sister, Carol McCartt, was her donor. Gil endured heavy chemo, which killed every cancerous cell, before the transplant. James told me of her courage: "I was a police officer, and I thought I knew courage. I was in Vietnam, and I thought I met courageous people. But I did not know courage until I watched her go through this."[6]

Nighttime was the worst. Too many sleepless hours thinking, hurting, staring at the ceiling. Gil relates, "There were many nights when I was down. I lay there praying hard. Every time I felt the worst, my childhood minister called me to pray. He prayed and I knew things were okay. I hung up, confident I could get through another night."[7]

Cancer forced Gil into greater dependence on God. Before cancer, she didn't really believe the Bible was literal, nor did she understand what people meant when they spoke of a "personal relationship" with God. But cancer drove her to deeper faith. She prayed more personally: "Okay, God, we are going to live life today. Can you help me breathe? I am getting a little panicked." She remains amazed that she could pray freely and sense God's presence.

Gil had plenty of time to study during her illness. At one time, she studied five hours a day while receiving medication. "I scared one friend to death," Gil says with a smile. "She was convinced I was becoming some sort of Bible freak. I used to look at those people like they had lost their minds. But God's Word became fascinating to me. I saw how it was practical and literal. It brought me amazing comfort. My disease accelerated my spiritual growth."[8]

Gil survived the stem-cell transplant and gradually re-entered life. In June of 2000 she returned to work, over a year and three months after cancer's floodwaters crashed into her life. Gil and James will never be the same.

After enduring this flood, Gil thinks more about mortality. Every day counts. She told me: "Time with my church has to count. Time with my kids has to count. Time with James has to count. If I get frustrated with silly things. My trial has had positive benefits. It helped me love my job more. I have served my church more. It makes me think these days are absolutely vital, and they are just this enormous gift. Had I never gotten the disease, I would never have that. This is a better way of living."[9]

Gil also described how to prepare for a flood: "Like Noah, determine what you have to do first. In his case, he had to build this boat. He couldn't get overwhelmed about the flood coming. He had to trust God and build this thing."[10]

Gil's husband, James, says a flood brings two choices. "I can watch this flood engulf me, or I can trust God and drive this peg in this hole. And then I get the next plank, and I hope and pray and trust that he will let me get this completed before the flood overtakes us. All you can do is get through the next test; drive the next peg."[11]

Both Gil and James exhibit a faith that floats, that sustains them on the roughest waters and through the darkest nights. They learned the truth of Oswald Chambers's words: "Faith means, whether I am visibly delivered or not, I will stick to my belief that God is love. There are some things only learned in a fiery furnace."[12] Gil and James learned to cherish each day and trust God with the rest. They learned to be thankful rather than angry, to live in the present instead of the past or future, and to love others in a richer way.

God promises:

> "When you pass through the waters,
>    I will be with you;
> and when you pass through the rivers,
>    they will not sweep over you.
> When you walk through the fire,
>    you will not be burned;
>    the flames will not set you ablaze.
> For I am the LORD, your God,
>    the Holy One of Israel, your Savior."
>
> ISAIAH 43:2–3

The text does not say "*if* you pass through the waters" or "*if* you walk through the fire," but *when*. We all face floods and storms; we all walk through fire. In those moments, trust God's strength and power, rest in his goodness and love. God is faithful. He can carry you as he did the Farrens.

## All I Ever Needed to Know I Learned from Noah

One person compiled some lessons entitled, "All I Ever Needed to Know I Learned from Noah."

1. Be prepared. It wasn't raining when Noah built the ark.
2. Stay fit. When you're six hundred years old, someone might ask you to do something REALLY BIG.
3. Don't listen to critics. Do what has to be done.
4. Build on high ground.
5. For safety's sake, travel in pairs.
6. Two heads are better than one.
7. Speed isn't always an advantage. The cheetahs were on board, but so were the snails.
8. If you can't fight or flee, float.
9. Take care of your animals as if they are the last ones on earth.
10. Don't forget that we're all in the same boat.
11. When the doo-doo gets deep, don't complain. SHOVEL.
12. Stay below deck during the storm.
13. Remember: The ark was built by amateurs; the *Titanic* was built by professionals.
14. If you have to start over, have a friend by your side.
15. Woodpeckers on the INSIDE are often a bigger threat than the storm outside.
16. Don't miss the boat.
17. No matter how bleak it looks, there's always a rainbow on the other side.[13]

Let's look at some practical things from Noah's example that can help us develop a faith that floats.

### Know God's Word

Do you remember the story of the three little pigs? Once upon a time there were three little pigs who decided to each build a house. The first little pig built his house out of straw, the second out of sticks, and the third out of bricks. One day, a big bad wolf knocked on the door of the first pig's house. "Little pig, little pig, let me in," he said.

The little pig replied, "Not by the hair of my chinny, chin, chin."

The wolf threatened, "Then I'll huff, and I'll puff, and I'll blow your house down." And he blew the straw house to pieces.

So the pig ran his little legs off to his friend's stick house. But the wolf showed up and blew that house to pieces. The pigs ran to the third pig's brick house. The wolf blew and blew, but the brick house stood because it had been built with wisdom.

Jesus tells a similar story.[14] He says:

"Therefore everyone who hears these words of mine and puts them into practice is like a wise man who built his house on the rock. The rain came down, the streams rose, and the winds blew and beat against that house; yet it did not fall, because it had its foundation on the rock. But everyone who hears these words of mine and does not put them into practice is like a foolish man who built his house on sand. The rain came down, the streams rose, and the winds blew and beat against that house, and it fell with a great crash."

MATTHEW 7:24–27

The flood comes to every house; the big bad wolf visits the door of each little pig. The question is: Will we build on a foundation that withstands the winds and floods?

God's Word is that foundation. Noah survived because he listened to God's word. Without God's word, he possessed no idea about the boat's dimensions or what to do when completing it. Noah received God's direct revelation; we receive God's revelation in the Bible.

The Bible is the best-selling book in history. Total sales exceed one billion dollars a year. But despite this sales record and longevity, how many consult the Bible for guidance? How many grasp its content?

Jay Leno and *The Tonight Show* performed on-the-street interviews with two college-age girls.

"Can you name one of the Ten Commandments?" Leno asked one.

"Freedom of speech," she answered.

"Complete this sentence," Leno said. "Let he who is without sin . . ."

"Have a good time?" she responded.

"Who, according to the Bible, was eaten by the whale?" Leno questioned.

"Pinocchio," she stated confidently.

We cannot stay afloat during floods unless we know God's Word and heed his warnings. Take some advice from D. L. Moody.

I prayed for faith, and thought that some day faith would come down and strike me like lightning. But faith did not seem to come. One day I read in the tenth chapter of Romans, "Now faith comes by hearing, and hearing by the Word of God." I had closed my Bible, and prayed for faith. I now opened my Bible, and began to study, and faith has been growing ever since."[15]

There are thirty-one chapters in the Book of Proverbs: Read a chapter a day for a month. Study the Gospels in the

New Testament: Matthew, Mark, Luke, and John. Take the three hours you would spend watching a movie and read God's Word instead. Find out for yourself what God has communicated to us.

### Obey God's Word

The Internet amazes me. I can log onto the Net and get directions to anywhere in the United States. Just for fun, I asked for directions from 1967 Broadway in New York City to my house in southern California. "Start out going south on Broadway toward W. 66th St. by turning right (0.1 miles)," the map states. Fifty-seven instructions later and the map leads right to my door. Total distance: 2,753.6 miles. Estimated time: 46 hours, 16 minutes. Maybe I'll try it someday—on a plane! It is one thing to have the map; it is another to take the trip. And it is one thing to know God's Word; it is another to obey it.

Noah knew God's word and obeyed his leading. But our temptation is to question God's Word rather than obey. The serpent deceived Eve in Eden by saying, "Did God really say, 'You must not eat from any tree in the garden?'" (Gen. 3:1). The serpent knew that causing Eve to question and doubt God's word would open her heart to disobedience.

We follow the serpent's line of justification when we say, "Did God really say I must forgive my enemies? Come on!" or "Did God really say I must not gossip? Isn't that a little extreme?" or "Did God really say I must abstain from sexual activity outside of marriage? We're getting married, so what's the difference?" Finding loopholes helps us justify our actions. But the issue is not interpretation. The issue is obedience.

Imagine Noah saying, "God, a big boat is so impractical. I think I heard you incorrectly. You meant 83 feet long, not 483, right? I'll build an 83 foot boat." Or imagine him saying, "Surely you don't want all the animals on the ark. That's outrageous! Some of these animals smell worse than others, and remember, we don't have plumbing! I'll just round up a few of my favorites. The others can tread water just fine." The effects would have been disastrous if Noah had disobeyed.

God commands us to treat others with kindness, to let our "yes be yes" and our "no be no," to love and serve others. There's no interpretation needed. God presented much of his Word to us in black and white. Our challenge is to follow through and obey. God's greatest blessings dwell on the other side of obedience. By obeying, we develop a faith that withstands floods.

### Stand in God's Righteousness

Floods make us aware of our faults and failures. During floods we are tempted to believe God does not care or that we are not forgiven. But we must remember we stand by *grace* in God's righteousness, even amidst storms and floods.

Genesis calls Noah "a righteous man, blameless among the people in his time" (Gen. 6:9). Hebrews says Noah "became heir of the righteousness that comes by faith" (Heb. 11:7). Noah's righteousness was not a result of extreme willpower, great effort, or self-help books. His righteousness was a result of faith.

Righteousness derives from a belief in God's sacrifice through Jesus. Spiritual ruts trap us when we judge everything in our spiritual lives by performance. But God's grace is not dictated by performance; it is unearned.

Paul says we have been "justified through faith, we have peace with God through our Lord Jesus Christ, through whom we have gained access by faith into this *grace in which we now stand*" (Rom. 5:1–2, emphasis added). We do not claw and fight for God's approval. Through faith, we possess it.

I will never forget coming home one hot Monday afternoon in May. I felt frustrated by my wife's insistence that I come home before another engagement I had to attend. Arriving, I noticed the flowerbed needed watering and the grass mowing—more things to do! As I walked in the door, she handed me a gift bag containing a bib which read, "I love Pooh and Daddy too." It took twenty seconds for the reality to hit me—I was going to be a dad! In the next few moments, my worldview altered. The flowerbed and lawn were the last things on my mind!

Several days later I heard some parenting tips on the radio. I thought, "That will be helpful to someone." Then it struck me: "That will be helpful to me!" What a sobering moment. My position in the world had changed. I was not only a husband; I was a father.

Placing faith in Christ changes our position. We are not the same as before. We are not only people, we are God's children. We are not only forgiven, we are righteous "in Christ." We are incorporated "into Christ." The phrases "in Christ," "in him," and "in the Lord" are used again and again in the New Testament. The term points to our change in position. To be "in Christ" is to abide in a deep and growing relationship with God. Our righteousness is found in him; our hope is found in him; our life is found in him.

No other religion offers this kind of personal union with its founder. The Buddhist does not claim to be "in Buddha"; those who admire Confucius do not aspire to be "in Confucius"; the Muslim is not "in Mohammed," nor the Marxist "in Karl Marx."

But the Christian is "in Christ." He or she unites with him and depends on him. Jesus lived perfectly—he achieved a perfect righteousness. Since we are in him, God looks at us and sees his Son. We are covered by Jesus' righteousness. Paul writes, "For it is by grace you have been saved, through faith—and this not from yourselves, it is the gift of God—not by works, so that no one can boast" (Eph. 2:8).

John Wesley grasped this grace when he was on the Atlantic's tide. On December 10, 1725, the *Simmonds* launched into open seas with 225 passengers. Their destination was Savannah, Georgia, and John and Charles Wesley traveled on the ship. The Oxford-trained John Wesley had founded the Methodist movement, and his "method" was very strict, including prayers, fasts, a rigorous examination of conscience, and good works. Each day he journaled about the trip's events.

Wesley rose daily at 4:00 A.M. for prayer. He continued with spiritual disciplines until 8:00 or 9:00 P.M. But something plagued him—the recurring fear of shipwreck that reduced his faith to nothing.

On January 17, a wave crashed into the ship and water penetrated the lower deck where John sat. His fear of death shocked him. On January 24, a huge wave knocked him down on deck. He expected to die. Later, he questioned himself: "How is it that thou hast no faith? Being still unwilling to die."

A group of Moravian Christians made him even more aware of his fear, because they were calm on the mighty ocean. They were not impressed with Wesley's spiritual disciplines—they viewed salvation as an unearned gift of grace. All of Wesley's effort appeared to them as another attempt to earn God's grace.

One Sunday evening a storm raged so fiercely that the ship sounded like it was splintering. John went to the Moravians' Sunday evening worship service. While everyone else on the ship panicked, the Moravians held hands to stable themselves, and they praised God. They rejoiced in God with firm and secure faith.

Wesley was taken aback. "Were you not afraid?" he asked a Moravian man after the storm.

"I thank God, no," the man responded.

"But were not your women and children afraid?" Wesley asked.

The man replied mildly, "No; our women and children are not afraid to die."[16]

This experience had a profound impact on Wesley. The Moravians' faith allowed them to overcome fear because their faith was not based on the shaky ground of human effort. With complete assurance, they rode the tides as "heirs of the righteousness that is *by faith* "

For several years, I tried to stand on my own righteousness with fasting, prayer, study, and service. I did good things for wrong reasons—to atone for past sins. I ran hard on the treadmill of human effort, but I eventually wore out. I felt desperate over my failure to achieve righteousness. Finally, I surrendered, and God moved powerfully. I realized in my heart that righteousness is by faith. Living out of that realization, I have changed for the better. Power, hope, and grace

81

flow freely from my life. When floods come, I don't beat myself up or blame myself; I allow the flood to help me develop perseverance. I trust God and ride the tides above the raging waters.

When rains come and the flood waters rise, remember your position in God's grace. Your sin is not too dark, your failures not too great, your mistakes not too overwhelming for God's grace. Reach out to him. No matter how big the waves or how furious the wind, God will support you. Your faith, like Noah's, will float.

Noah remains the ultimate tide rider, standing as a beacon of light, pointing us toward faith. As you pick up your own tools and obey God's call, you too can experience the joy of being carried along in his power. In a spiritual sense, throw the oars and rudders overboard. Surrender the direction of your life to God. Get in the ark. Trust the wind of his Spirit to carry you along above the flood waters.

# FIVE

# A FAITH THAT FOLLOWS GOD'S VISION

*Faith does not operate in the realm of the possible. There is no glory for God in that which is humanly possible. Faith begins where man's power ends.*[1]

GEORGE MÜLLER

Rob stared in amazement at the note on his guitar case. For years, he and his wife, Shannon, had sensed a call to the mission field, but no opportunities had seemed right. A few months earlier, a large missions organization offered Rob a position. He felt excited and ready, but Shannon had no peace, so Rob painfully surrendered the dream. He re-signed himself to supporting missions within the church where he served as a youth minister. But suddenly this note on his guitar case changed everything.

The events leading to that note occurred at a high school summer camp in 1999, as Rob conversed with Kevin Dooley, president of FAME (Fellowship of Associates of Medical Evangelism). They talked about the lack of collegiate internships where American students could get college credit for field experience and learning in missions. Mexico City seemed like one of the best host cities for interns on the field because it was cheap to get there and filled with two million university students. Most parents felt fairly comfortable sending their children to Mexico as opposed to other places.

Kevin's eyes lit up during their talk. "This is a God conversation," he said.

"Don't even start with that stuff," Rob replied. "I'm not interested."

"I think you're the guy God is calling to do this."

"No way! I'm just not interested." The last time Rob thought God was calling him to mission work, Shannon did not, and Rob had been deeply disappointed.

"I'm serious; I think God is in this," Kevin countered.

When Rob left the conversation, he prayed, "God, if you are talking to me, talk to my wife first. If you aren't talking to her, I'm not listening."

An hour and a half later, Rob entered the camp chapel and saw the note on his guitar case.

Rob,
I just want you to know that I will serve wherever God wants us to go. If that means somewhere other than here, I'm ready to go. I sense God's calling to missions in a powerful way.
    I love you,
    Shannon[2]

A lump rose in his throat. What was God doing? While he had been talking about Mexico City with Kevin Dooley, Shannon had sensed God's call to Mexico City and took up her pen and wrote, "I'm ready to go." They were being called to serve as overseas missionaries.

Shannon remembers, "The most incredible thing is that God called us both. He didn't just tell Rob; he also made it clear to me."[3] When they drove away from camp, they knew their lives would never be the same.

They committed to pray, fast, and seek God's direction over the next month. Time and again, God confirmed their call to Mexico. Their vision to mobilize students and build better relationships between short term and host mis sionaries developed.

Seeing a vision is one thing; experiencing its fulfillment is another. Rob and Shannon had no clue how to arrive in Mexico City with mission support. Rob needed a master's degree to host American students for college credit, but he didn't know how to pay for it or how to connect with the right people in Mexico City. But step by step, God opened one door after another.

Rob resigned from his youth ministry in order to begin graduate school. He received a large grant from the school, and missions support came. God always managed the details. For instance, their home sold before they even put it on the market. Rob received an invitation to a Christ in Youth conference in Mexico City, where he made needed contacts. As they stepped out in faith, God made their vision a reality.

God called Rob and Shannon to leave family, friends, environment, and security. He challenged them to step across the boundary of the known for the unknown, the seen for the unseen, the possible for the impossible. He asked them to give up their home and their paycheck and to exchange one ministry for another. He beckoned them to ride faith's tides.

Today, Rob and Shannon, along with two other couples, serve in Mexico City. Rob does not know how long he will serve there or what the future holds, but he trusts God's leadership. God has expanded their horizons, pushed their boundaries, and forced them outside of their boxes. Rob and Shannon are living the extraordinary life, pursuing their God-given vision.

God gives us the capacity to dream and develop visions for our lives. A vision operates like a compass helping direct our choices and decisions. Vision allows dreams to materialize and become reality. Developing a vision takes time, prayer, and wise counsel, but it makes a tremendous difference. When we connect our vision with God's vision, we accomplish so much more in life.

Abel reminds us to leave a legacy, Enoch inspires us to faithwalk, and Noah challenges us to obey. Abraham's life teaches us to follow God's vision across boundaries. Webster defines a boundary as "anything marking a limit." Abraham lived on the limit between the known and the unknown, the seen and the unseen. He learned that faith, as Corrie ten Boom put it, "sees the invisible, believes the unbelievable, and receives the impossible."[4]

## Living beyond the Boundary of the Known

Abraham was the father of the Jewish race and the father of faith, but he was no desert monk. He probably worshiped multiple gods before worshiping the one God.

86

He had a family, an army, wealth, and plenty of comforts. But, like Rob and Shannon, Abraham was forced out of his comfort zone, and he experienced God's power. Hebrews reads:

> By faith Abraham, when called to go to a place he would later receive as his inheritance, obeyed and went, even though he did not know where he was going. By faith he made his home in the promised land like a stranger in a foreign country; he lived in tents, as did Isaac and Jacob, who were heirs with him of the same promise. For he was looking forward to the city with foundations, whose architect and builder is God.
>
> HEBREWS 11:8–10

Abraham began the life of faith with a journey. He lived in Ur of the Chaldeans, a thriving metropolis, and God told him, "'Leave your country, your people and your father's household and go to the land I will show you'" (Gen. 12:1). God challenged him to step out in faith across the boundary of the known into the unknown.[5]

Hebrews says Abraham obeyed when called; he followed God's vision to a whole new world. The original language implies that Abraham literally packed his bags while being called. He left Ur, the city of the world, for Canaan, the land of promise. He hit the road "even though he did not know where he was going" (Heb. 11:8).

Though Abraham obeyed, he made an incomplete break with his past. God commanded him to leave his father's household, but Tarah, his father, and his nephew, Lot, traveled along. They journeyed to Haran, where they lived fifteen years until his father died. Then Abraham headed

87

southwest into the wilderness. His obedience was imperfect, but by God's grace he moved in the right spiritual direction.

Abraham's faith remained deeply personal and grounded in an experience with the living God. As Brennan Manning writes, Abraham's faith

> is a paradigm of all authentic faith. It is a movement into obscurity, into the undefined, into ambiguity, and not into some predetermined, clearly delineated plan for the future. Each future determination, each next step discloses itself only out of a discernment of the influence of God in the present moment.[6]

Responding to God, we cross the boundary of the known into the unknown. All great people of faith crossed this boundary. Noah built an ark without seeing a drop of rain. Daniel stepped into the lion's den. Shadrach, Meshach, and Abednego walked into the fire. Paul regularly changed plans and directions. These people did not know how things would turn out; they were not sure if they would survive. But they did know that God was leading them, and that remained enough. They understood, as Oswald Chambers did, that "faith in God is a terrific venture in the dark."[7]

We often struggle with God's plan and direction. We desire to see everything laid out nicely and neatly—where we will work, whom we will marry, what we will experience. We can develop visions for these areas of our lives, but our security is in knowing who leads the trip.

Maybe you recently graduated from college and you're nervous about post-college life. Maybe you sense God's leading into full-time ministry, but you can't see how this will be financially possible. Maybe you were laid off and the future is in disarray. Reach out and take God's hand. Step over the boundary into the unknown and let his tide of love and grace carry you. The life of faith is lived on a need-to-know basis.

When we lead visionary lives, we have a dual tension. On one hand, we live with a God-given picture of our future; we pursue his call on our lives. On the other hand, God's time frame may be entirely different than ours. We must learn to trust, wait, pray, and watch.

When we struggle with the unknown aspects in our lives, the most important question to ask is: Who do I want to please? If I desire to please God and grow closer to him, I cannot be lost. Thomas Merton captured this sentiment.

> My Lord God, I have no idea where I am going. I do not see the road ahead of me. I cannot know for certain where it will end. Nor do I really know myself, and the fact that I think I am following your will does not mean that I am actually doing so. But I believe that the desire to please you does in fact please you.[8]

I find great hope knowing that my desire to please God does please him.

## Living beyond the Boundary of the Seen

Stepping over the boundary of the known, Abraham caught a vision of God's people and God's city. To fully grasp the vision, he crossed another boundary—the boundary of the seen into the unseen. He lived on the basis of unseen realities.

God revealed a picture of Abraham's vision, saying:

89

"Look up at the heavens and count the stars—if indeed you can count them." Then he said to him, "So shall your offspring be."

Abram believed the Lord, and he credited it to him as righteousness.

He also said to him, "I am the Lord, who brought you out of Ur of the Chaldeans to give you this land to take possession of it."

Genesis 15:5–7

Hebrews says the vision was greater than offspring and land. Abraham and the ancients endured because they saw the bigger picture. "All these people were still living by faith when they died" says Hebrews.

They did not receive the things promised; they only saw them and welcomed them from a distance. And they admitted that they were aliens and strangers on earth. People who say such things show that they are looking for a country of their own. If they had been thinking of the country they had left, they would have had opportunity to return. Instead, *they were longing for a better country—a heavenly one*. Therefore God is not ashamed to be called their God, for he has prepared a city for them.

Hebrews 11:13–16, emphasis added

Abel, Enoch, Noah, Abraham, and other ancients stepped across the line of the seen, despite receiving promises that were unrealized in their lifetimes. They followed, looking forward to the heavenly city, the new Jerusalem. They lived with vision.

It is possible that we may spend our lives laying the groundwork for a vision that is fulfilled after our death. How many missionaries died with little fruit, only to influ-

90

ence thousands after their death? God's vision is fulfilled God's way. This means we must be careful about our focus. If the ancients had focused on the seen, they would have gotten discouraged and frustrated. But instead they focused on the vision.

God called Abraham to leave Ur, the place to be if you were moving up in the world. The land surrounding Ur, however, was a bare, dirty desert. To survive in the desert, Abraham looked in the right spiritual direction and saw the unseen.

I owned a Fiero in high school. It was a sporty, red two-door with a black stripe down the side. One day as I was driving a busy street, I noticed joggers on the opposite side of the road. Having focused on them, I crashed into an abandoned station wagon. I wasn't wearing a seat belt and was traveling at a speed of forty-five miles per hour. Music blared from my car stereo as I picked glass out of my ear. Thankfully, I walked away from the accident, and learned that it's dangerous to stop looking in the right direction.

This also applies to our spiritual lives. When we take our focus off God and his unseen promises, we travel a crash course that wreaks havoc in our lives. Paul says, "Since, then, you have been raised with Christ, *set your hearts on things above*, where Christ is seated at the right hand of God. *Set your minds on things above*, not on earthly things" (Col. 3:1–2, emphasis added). We can endure anything when we focus on things above.

Those who achieve the most in this life focus on the next! Keep looking forward toward the new heaven, the new earth, and God's amazing blessing. There is light at the end of the tunnel. There is hope beyond despair. There is love,

91

freedom, and healing. Live like Abraham on the basis of unseen realities.

## Living beyond the Boundary of the Possible

Abraham received a promise—he saw the vision that his descendants would outnumber the stars. The only problem: His wife, Sarah, remained barren. Years had passed since God first told Abraham he would have descendants. Abraham had to learn the patience of faith the hard way. Hebrews says:

> By faith Abraham, even though he was past age—and Sarah herself was barren—was enabled to become a father because he considered him faithful who had made the promise. And so from this one man, and he as good as dead, came descendants as numerous as the stars in the sky and as countless as the sand on the seashore.
>
> HEBREWS 11:11–12

At ninety-nine years old Abraham was told to change Sarai's name to Sarah (princess) because she would bear a son and become the mother of many nations. "Abraham fell facedown; he laughed and said to himself, 'Will a son be born to a man a hundred years old? Will Sarah bear a child at the age of ninety?'" (Gen. 17:17).

Though properly facedown, Abraham laughed at the impossibility. Sarah had aged. Time had passed. When Sarah heard three mysterious guests tell Abraham that she would soon be a mother, she "laughed to herself as she thought, 'After I am worn out and my master is old, will I now have this pleasure?'" (Gen. 18:12). Sarah probably

92

thought, "Great! Now that I'm an old lady, God blesses me with children—yeah right!" She could not help but laugh.

God said to Abraham, "'Why did Sarah laugh and say, "Will I really have a child now that I am old?" Is anything too hard for the Lord?'" (Gen. 18:13–14). Can't you hear Abraham's reply? "God, it's not possible. I'm one hundred years old, and my wife is ninety! What in the world are you doing?" My mom was forty and my dad forty-five when I invaded their retirement plans. They thought my conception was impossible. Imagine being ninety! Sarah was probably way past menopause. Envision this ninety-year-old woman with morning sickness, shopping for maternity clothes. Yet her dreams were fulfilled because nothing is impossible for God.

Many God-given visions are fulfilled over long periods of waiting. Abraham and Sarah waited twenty-four years for the promise of a child to be fulfilled. The Israelites waited four hundred years before they actually left Egypt to take the Promised Land. Moses and the Israelites waited forty years in the desert before crossing the Jordan. The patience of faith is extremely difficult, but God forms us as we wait. He molds us into his image.

Many begin the Christian life with a vision or dream of using their gifts. When that dream gets squelched, stepped on, or doesn't occur in an expected time frame, these Christians stop waiting for the impossible. But faith waits and believes. Henri Nouwen offered a moving picture of faith. He wrote of trapeze artists traveling with a circus called The Flying Rodleys. The trapeze artists told him of the special relationship between the flyer, who releases the bar and soars through the air, and the catcher. The flyer maintains absolute faith in the catcher. He extends his arms and holds perfect form as he falls. If he tries to catch the catcher or if he panics or breaks form, the situation could be disastrous. Instead he waits until the strong arms of the catcher snatch him from the air. That is a powerful image of faith.[9] When plans fail and dreams get sidetracked, we want to panic, but we must wait on the catcher. Even when free-falling, we must trust that God, the great catcher, will catch us.

Maybe you want to accomplish a certain task, but year after year the door remains closed. Maybe you understand your vision in life, but God keeps applying the brakes. Wait for the catcher to catch you. Don't surrender the vision God places on your heart and don't let failure destroy your dreams. The first comment I heard after preaching my first message was "You have the whitest teeth I have ever seen." I thought, "Thanks, I'm glad to know this changed your life!" (I hope I have improved a little!) But I didn't surrender my dream of being a pastor after an initial failure.

Langston Hughes challenged, "Hold fast to dreams, for if dreams die, life is a broken-winged bird that cannot fly." Every tide rider fails—multiple times! Every faithwalker is challenged. You may wait weeks or decades, but God is faithful. If your vision is in line with his call, it will come to pass, during your lifetime or after. Cross the line of the possible to the impossible.

## Living beyond the Boundary of Sacrifice

Faith's walk always involves a cost. Visions are tested. Abraham came to understand this reality in a unique way. Hebrews says:

By faith Abraham, when God tested him, offered Isaac as a sacrifice. He who had received the promises was about to sacrifice his one and only son, even though God had said to him, "It is through Isaac that your offspring will be reckoned." Abraham reasoned that God could raise the dead, and figuratively speaking, he did receive Isaac back from death.

Hebrews 11:17–19

I can't imagine Abraham's horror when he was asked to sacrifice his only son. This went against all his natural instincts, all his inclinations, all his dreams. Isaac was the promised child they had waited for all their lives. Now God required his life. How could this be? How could God do such a thing?

Abraham knew God had spoken, so at dawn the next morning, without a word to Sarah, he departed with Isaac, two servants, and a saddled donkey. It was a three-day journey to Mount Moriah— probably the longest three days of Abraham's life. When he reached the mountain's base, he told the servants to wait while he and Isaac worshiped. Isaac addressed him affectionately as *Abba*, or Daddy. "'The fire and wood are here,' Isaac said, 'but where is the lamb for the burnt offering?' Abraham answered, 'God himself will provide the lamb for the burnt offering, my son.' And the two of them went on together" (Gen. 22:7–8). Who can fathom the turmoil going through Abraham's mind? Who can understand what he felt or thought? He had crossed the boundary of sacrifice.

Perhaps Isaac lay down, allowing his father to tie him. Maybe Abraham used force. The verb tense describing Abraham's sacrifice points to completed action in past time. He had already taken Isaac's life as far as his obedience was concerned.[10] So he raised the knife to take his child's life.

95

But the angel of the Lord called out to him from heaven,
"Abraham! Abraham!"
"Here I am," he replied.
"Do not lay a hand on the boy," he said. "Do not do anything to him. Now I know that you fear God, because you
have not withheld from me your son, your only son."
Abraham looked up and there in a thicket he saw a ram
caught by its horns. He went over and took the ram and
sacrificed it as a burnt offering instead of his son.

Genesis 22:11–13

God intervened in a miraculous way and provided for
the sacrifice! Abraham passed the test. He truly surrendered
everything.

Anne Lamott wrote of how her own conversion origi-
nated in Abraham's amazing story of sacrifice.

In the interior silence that followed my understanding of
this scene, I held my breath for as long as I could, sitting
there under the fluorescent lights—and then I crossed over.
I don't know how else to put it or how and why I actively
made, if not exactly a *leap* of faith, a lurch of faith. . . . I
left class believing—accepting—that there was a God. I did
not understand how this could have happened. It made
no sense. It made no sense that what brought me to this
conviction was the story of a God who would ask his
beloved Abraham to sacrifice the child he loved more than
life itself. It made no sense that Abraham could head for
the mountain in Moriah still believing in God's goodness.
It made no sense that even as he walked his son to the sacrificial altar, he still believed God's promise that Isaac would
give him many descendants. It made no sense that he was
willing to do the one thing in the world he could not do,
just because God told him to. God told him to obey and to
believe that he was a loving God and could be trusted. So
Abraham did obey. I felt changed and a little crazy. But

96

though I was still like a stained and slightly buckled jigsaw puzzle with some pieces missing, now there were at least a few border pieces in place.[11]

The power of Abraham's incredible faith, this unbelievable willingness to give up the most important thing in his life, astounded Lamott as it astounds me. It points me to something beyond, to the one who was willing to sacrifice his Son, Jesus, on the cross. It points me to the amazing sacrifice of faith.

Faith's path is one of dying to our agendas, our goals, our aspirations, and instead, living for God's will. As Jesus said, "Whoever finds his life will lose it, and whoever loses his life for my sake will find it" (Matt. 10:39). Those who live the life of faith are in many ways like dead men and women walking. They have died to themselves, and in that death, they experience the resurrection life of Jesus. As Martin Luther said when he preached on Abraham's sacrifice, "We say, 'In the midst of life we die.' God answers, 'Nay, in the midst of death we live.'"[12]

Living beyond the boundary of sacrifice fills us with joy in riding faith's tides. We experience life on the edge, a life filled with new horizons and unexpected turns.

## Vision beyond Boundaries

Abraham began faith's journey by stepping into the unknown and leaving Ur. Jonathan Swift said, "Vision is the art of seeing things invisible." When you look to the future, what do you see? Consider these questions about your personal vision.

*What pictures do you see for your future?* The way we view our future is more important than the way we view our present or our past. We must be able to envision the future before we achieve it. Develop a picture of what could be and work toward that with prayer and planning. Write out a description or draw a picture of what you see in your future in the areas of faith, marriage/family, work, and finances. Pray about these areas and seek God's plan.

*Is your vision in line with God's Word?* We must determine that our personal visions are not going against the grain of God's revealed will for our lives. As we study God's Word, we can begin to understand that our primary purpose in life is to glorify him and serve him forever. Does your vision restrict you from doing this? Can it enhance your ability to glorify God?

*Do you have a passion for this vision?* No vision comes to fruition without passion, sacrifice, and dedication. Passion is key in determining the direction of our hearts. One way to determine your passion is to look at your prayers. What consumes your prayer life?

*Do you have the potential to achieve this vision with God's help?* We have to take an honest inventory of our gifts and abilities. For instance, if you are slow and frail, professional football probably won't be on your list! Assess your potential honestly, but don't be quick to answer negatively. The question is not "Can you achieve it now?" The question is, "Do I have the potential to achieve it with God's help, hard work, and dedication?"

I have a card from my parents that reads, "Edmund Hillary stood at the edge of the stage, made a fist, and pointed at a picture of the mountain. He said in a loud voice 'You beat me the first time, but I'll beat you the next time because you've grown all you are going to grow . . . but I'm still growing!' A year later, he succeeded in becoming the first man to climb Mount Everest." As important as that message is, the message my parents wrote on the inside of the card is even more important: "God first. Family next. Then the church as a body. Believe in yourself the way we believe in you."

God often calls us to tasks greater than what we can do on our own. God calls us to God-sized tasks. We must believe in God and believe in ourselves. When he calls us to a task, he gives us resources to complete it.

Rob and Shannon laid it all on the line for their vision, and they have found God faithful. Rob said, "When the knife goes down, you feel it. Anybody who tells you otherwise has not sacrificed. The day we drove away from our church, our family, and our friends was a knife in my heart. But, on the other side of sacrifice, God's grace is magnificent. In reality, we have not sacrificed, we have been privileged to participate in God's vision for our lives and Mexico City. The riches we gained in walking by faith is that God has made himself more real to us. By trusting him and cutting our ties, the reward has been more of him. And we would never trade that!"[13]

If we surrender to God in faith, we will be amazed at how he moves limitations and boundaries. Genesis tells us that Abraham lived 175 years. "And Abraham breathed his last and died in a ripe old age, an old man and satisfied with life; and he was gathered to his people" (Gen. 25:7–8 NASB). What could be better than reaching the end of our days "satisfied with life"? God holds blessing for those who live like Abraham, like Rob and Shannon, those who live in faith beyond the boundaries.

# SIX

# A FAITH THAT CHOOSES
# GOD'S WILL

*The word upon which all adventure, all exhilaration,
all meaning, all honor depends. In the beginning was
the word and the word was CHOICE.*[1]

TOM ROBBINS

When I was growing up, I loved playing the electric
guitar. Like millions of other teenagers, my dream
was to be a rock star. I even moved to Albuquerque after
high school to join a band. Though my love was electric
guitar, I played bass. Our band's name: Angelic Force. Talk
about the eighties! This was the era of big hair, spandex,
and heavy metal. And, yes, I wore spandex. It was not a

pretty picture! We played a few concerts and some of our songs got radio airplay. We had a blast, even though the videotapes of those concerts are now quite embarrassing.

All through my experience with the band I felt an inner tug—I could not bury it; I could not escape it. God was calling me to attend a Christian college in Dallas. He confirmed it continually, but I lived in denial. I had to choose between two paths: the band or Bible college. In hindsight, this decision may appear small, but in the moment it constituted a huge choice of faith. I related to Robert Frost's famous poem, "The Road Not Taken."

> Two roads diverged in a yellow wood,
> And sorry I could not travel both
> And be one traveler, long I stood.

I struggled with God's will, searched his Word, prayed, and sought wise counsel. My heart remained with the band, but God called me to the college. So with tears, I surrendered, packed, and headed home to attend Bible college.

Each one of us faces choices. Sometimes those choices appear easy; sometimes they seem difficult. Sometimes they are based on clear direction; sometimes they are confusing. Our temptation is to base choices on what we see, taste, touch, hear, and smell. But if we walk with God, a whole new dimension emerges, because he rules the unseen. Faith often complicates our choices. When we live only for ourselves, our criteria for a choice involves our momentary whims. But walking with God requires many extra considerations. What does God desire me to do? How do I know God's will? How can I be sure I am making the right decision?

The vast majority of my life decisions involve prayer, patience, and action without an absolutely clear sense of God's direction. I move forward and God opens and closes doors. I seek obedience in clear moral areas revealed in Scripture and trust God to guide in the gray areas. I walk in faith. God gives guidance as guidance is needed.

Attending Bible college seemed difficult at first. The last thing I wanted to be was a minister. Between rock star or minister, which would you choose? But today I can do nothing else. Paul Little insightfully wrote:

> The will of God is not like a magic package let down from heaven by a string. . . . The will of God is far more like a scroll that unrolls every day. . . . The will of God is something to be discerned and lived out every day of our lives. It is not something to be grasped as a package once for all. Our call, therefore, is basically not to follow a plan or a blueprint, or go to a place or take up a work, but rather to follow the Lord Jesus Christ.[2]

Following Christ brings direction each day.

Fulfilling a vision is a result of daily choices of obedience to God's will. Those who live extraordinarily are not the most talented but the most available. They are not the most powerful but the most servant-oriented. They are not the most driven but the most surrendered. They choose God's will in spite of their own. They choose God's power when they are weak and worn. They take the road less traveled and experience faith's transforming power.

Moses would understand a fork in the road. As he followed God, he made choices of faith that incredibly impacted the world. He models the choices and experiences of a tide rider.

## God's Way

Moses' story begins with his parents' legacy of faith. Moses was born in Egypt. The Egyptians were kind to the Israelites in the days of Joseph. But by Moses' time, the mood had changed, and the pharaoh of the land oppressed the Israelites. "'Look,' [Pharaoh] said to his people, 'the Israelites have become much too numerous for us. Come, we must deal shrewdly with them or they will become even more numerous and, if war breaks out, will join our enemies, fight against us and leave the country'" (Exod. 1:9–10). So the king ordered the genocide of infant Israelites. He said to his people, "'Every boy that is born you must throw into the Nile, but let every girl live'" (Exod. 1:22).

Moses' parents, Amram and Jochebed, made a choice of faith. They "hid [Moses] for three months after he was born, because they saw he was no ordinary child, and they were not afraid of the king's edict" (Heb. 11:23). Amram and Jochebed knew God valued life, and they tried to rescue their child. They understood their responsibility to God came before their responsibility to the government.

As we consider God's will, we understand there is both an ultimate will of God (that we know him) and a moral will of God. He laid out clear moral laws in the Bible on how to think, what to value, and how to act. Amram and Jochebed knew that genocide went against God's moral will. In the times we live in now, we often skip past the moral dimension. I have counseled many couples who justify a divorce by saying, "God revealed to me that it is his will I get a divorce." These are not marriages with extreme physical or mental abuse, but marriages in which one party is convinced God desires a split. However, God's moral will remains clear

104

in Scripture; he says, "I hate divorce" (Mal. 2:16). He does not hate divorced people, but he hates what divorce does in people's lives. He hates the havoc and the pain it creates. He hates the way it breaks hearts and permanently separates relationships. God's specific plan for our lives does not violate his moral will. When we face a decision, one of our first questions should be: "Does this violate God's revealed moral will in Scripture?" This can clear up many issues.

Though we are called to be loyal to those governing us, this does not mean we should submit blindly. For instance, in Acts, Peter and John were commanded by the religious leaders not to speak in Jesus' name. "But Peter and John replied, 'Judge for yourselves whether it is right in God's sight to obey you rather than God. For we cannot help speaking about what we have seen and heard'" (Acts 4:19–20). Hundreds of years earlier, King Nebuchadnezzar issued an edict that his people were to worship a golden image. When they "heard the sound of the horn, flute, zither, lyre, harp and all kinds of music, all the peoples, nations and men of every language fell down and worshiped the image of gold that King Nebuchadnezzar had set up" (Dan. 3:7). But Shadrach, Meshach, and Abednego refused, claiming, "'O king . . . we will not serve your gods or worship the image of gold you have set up'" (Dan. 3:18).

Our loyalty to the government does not supercede our loyalty to God. Amram and Jochebed obeyed God because they "were not afraid of the king's edict" (Heb. 11:23). Fear has tremendous power. Fear drives us to do certain things and avoid doing others. "The remarkable thing," writes Oswald Chambers, ". . . is that when you fear God you fear nothing else, whereas if you do not fear God you fear everything else."[3] Fearing God involves recognizing that his awesome power exceeds any king's, his authority overrides any ruler's, his plan stands after everything collapses. Jesus said, "I tell you, my friends, do not be afraid of those who kill the body and after that can do no more. But I will show you whom you should fear: Fear him who, after the killing of the body, has power to throw you into hell. Yes, I tell you, fear him" (Luke 12:4–5).

Amram and Jochebed feared God; therefore, they feared no one else. They placed their trust in God's strong hands and hid the baby for three months. Still, their questions must have been relentless: Will the authorities find our boy today? Tomorrow? What will they do to us? Will this baby ever grow old?

Moses' parents had little going for them; they were slaves without money or material wealth and could not hide the baby forever. So after doing all they could, they put the baby in a papyrus basket coated with tar and pitch and placed it in the Nile among the reeds. They entrusted him to God's care. All they could do was wait, hope, and pray.

When they pushed the basket down the Nile, God's amazing plan unfolded. The basket floated to the place where Pharaoh's daughter bathed. She looked in the basket's direction and took notice. Sending her slave to get the basket, she discovered a beautiful child, and God moved her heart toward the baby.

Miriam, Moses' big sister, was standing on the bank when Pharaoh's daughter discovered Moses. So Miriam said to Pharaoh's daughter, "Shall I find a Hebrew woman to nurse him for you?"

She replied, "Yes, do you know one?"

Miriam answered, "Yes, I just happen to know one."

Miriam went home and said, "Mom, the princess just picked up our baby. She's looking for a nanny; will you apply for the job?" Jochebed applied and got the job, a paid position.

In 1998 *U.S. News and World Report* concluded that "the typical child in a middle-income family requires a 22-year investment of just over $1.45 million."[4] Imagine having someone pay *you* to raise your child—now snap out of it; you have bills to pay! This was not a bad deal for Jochebed!

Amram and Jochebed possessed a little basket and a lot of faith. But they also had a big, big God who revealed his power. Because Moses' parents chose God's will, Moses' education was funded by the very person who had called for his death.

You may feel like an underdog. You may not have financial leverage or social power. But you do have a big, big God who loves underdogs. Look at what he did with a papyrus basket and a choice of faith!

## The Greater Wealth

Egypt was the most cultured, educated, wealthy environment in the world. Moses grew up in Pharaoh's court and was a prince of Egypt for forty years. Imagine being raised as a prince in the wealthiest nation on earth. "Moses," says Stephen, "was educated in all the learning of the Egyptians, and he was a man of power in words and deeds" (Acts 7:22 NASB).

But at age forty he faced a choice. The Egyptians asked for full-fledged commitment: Would he be Egyptian or Hebrew? Due to his mother's influence, he understood his past. He knew the Hebrew language and God's ways. Would Moses give up comfort? People waited on his every need. Would he give up power? He did whatever he chose. Would he give up reputation? He commanded respect. Would he give up popularity? Any girl would love to marry him. Would he give up financial security? Egypt's riches were mind-boggling in proportion. Could he walk away from it all?

The issue was not simply one of wealth or influence. Joseph, Daniel, and others in the Bible had worked in powerful courts and had been surrounded by affluence. The issue was that "by faith" Moses knew God was calling him to choose. Hebrews tells us what he did:

> By faith Moses, when he had grown up, refused to be known as the son of Pharaoh's daughter. He chose to be mistreated along with the people of God rather than to enjoy the pleasures of sin for a short time. He regarded disgrace for the sake of Christ as of greater value than the treasures of Egypt, because he was looking ahead to his reward.
>
> HEBREWS 11:24–26

Refusing to be known as a "son of Pharaoh" meant renouncing all claims to Egyptian power and prestige. It meant joining the poor, dirty Hebrews—the slave people.

We often face Moses' questions: Will we sell out for prestige, power, and money? Will we allow other things to take precedence before God? Our choices may not necessarily involve giving up prestige, power, or money, because these things are not inherently evil. The evil is in making worldly choices over godly choices because of greed for money, power, and prestige. James reminds us that "Friendship with the world is hatred toward God" (James 4:4).

108

We are often tempted to make worldly choices. Maybe it's crossing ethical lines at work; maybe it's skimming a little money off the top; maybe it's flirting with an affair; maybe it's drugs or alcohol. When we are tempted to do these things, what values will we choose?

Moses chose ill treatment with God's people over the "passing pleasures of sin" (Heb. 11:25 NASB). Sin looks good because it feeds our appetites and desires. But there are consequences to pay once the pleasure passes—and it always passes. Moses "regarded disgrace for the sake of Christ as of greater value than the treasures of Egypt" (Heb. 11:26). Moses had a different value system. He viewed things through a different pair of lenses. He had experienced unlimited wealth and knew it could not satisfy.

Money and riches do not bring lasting happiness. Perhaps this is why VH1 voters nominated the Rolling Stones' song, "(I Can't Get No) Satisfaction" as the song of the millennium. We pour money, resources, time, and effort into finding satisfaction, yet it eludes us.

Malcolm Muggeridge was a twentieth century journalist who traveled the length and breadth of the world and lived very comfortably as editor of *Punch* magazine in England. Later in life, Muggeridge realized that all the world's wealth can't compare to the riches of Christ. He wrote in *Jesus Rediscovered:*

> I may, I suppose, regard myself, or pass for being, a relatively successful man. People occasionally stare at me in the streets—that's fame. I can fairly easily earn enough to qualify for admission to the highest slopes of the Internal Revenue—that's success. Furnished with money and a little fame even the elderly, if they care to, may partake of trendy diversions—that's pleasure. It might happen

once in a while that something I said or wrote was suffi-
ciently heeded for me to persuade myself that it repre-
sented a serious impact on our time—that's fulfillment.
Yet I say to you—and beg you to believe me—multiply
these tiny triumphs by a million, add them all together, and
they are nothing—less than nothing, a positive impedi-
ment—measured against one draught of that living water
Christ offers to the spiritually thirsty, irrespective of who
or what they are.[5]

Muggeridge, like Moses before him, realized that only God
truly satisfies!

## In the Desert, but Not Deserted

Before we polish up Moses and set him on a pedestal,
we must remember that he remained sinful. He committed murder, among other things. When Moses grew angry
with an Egyptian slave master who was beating a Hebrew
slave, he killed the slave master in rage. Fearing for his life,
Moses fled to the desert, which he roamed for forty years.
His dreams faded. He felt like a failure. He had gone from
the courts of Pharaoh to no-man's-land, from privilege to
menial labor as a shepherd, from popularity to anonymity.
But although Moses lived in the desert, God had not
deserted him.

We often speak of faith in terms of renewal, power, and
fulfillment, but rarely do we speak in terms of the desert.
Without the desert, Moses would have been unprepared
to lead. He needed the desert's lessons.

I have endured periods of barrenness when I have not
been able to sense God's presence. I prayed, read my Bible,
did acts of service, but experienced nothing. In retrospect,

I can see that the dryness resulted in great maturity. I grew in ways I could not have grown without it. I learned patience the hard way. My will was crushed and I was forced to submit to the timing and power of God. My weaknesses rose to the surface in undeniable ways, challenging me to deal with them. In general, the desert revealed my frailty and my desperate need for God. When I was in the desert, the externals I often diverted myself with lost their ability to satisfy and distract. Broken, I acknowledged a radical dependence on God. As St. John of the Cross said, "It was a happy chance that God should lead the soul into this night from which there came to it so much good." God can bring great good out of the dark times.

Many spiritual giants experienced times in the desert. David's perspective alters from psalm to psalm; some psalms are cries of a heart overwhelmed by God's absence. Job knew the way of the desert, as did Jeremiah and others.

In the midst of Moses' desert, God revealed his presence. Moses had woken up thousands of mornings in the desert. Little did he know that one such morning would change his life forever. God had prepared him. The time had arrived. God visited Moses in a burning bush.

Bushes burned in the desert, but this bush did not burn up. Moses walked toward it, and God proclaimed:

> "Moses! Moses! . . . Do not come any closer. . . . Take off your sandals, for the place where you are standing is holy ground. . . . I am the God of your father, the God of Abraham, the God of Isaac and the God of Jacob. . . . I am sending you to Pharaoh to bring my people the Israelites out of Egypt."
>
> Exodus 3:5–6, 10

111

Moses asked who was sending him, and God replied, "I AM WHO I AM. This is what you are to say to the Israelites: 'I AM has sent me to you'" (Exod. 3:14).

Moses needed a fresh perspective of God's power in that down-and-out moment. He needed to realize that though he had given up, God had not given up on him. In suffering or in difficult circumstances, we, like Moses, must cling to God's character. In failure and hopelessness, we must visit the burning bush and experience God. Corrie ten Boom said, "When a train goes through a tunnel and it gets dark, you don't throw away your ticket and jump off. You sit still and trust the engineer."[6] God is the engineer, the great I AM, the beginning and the end, the first and the last, the author of life and the conqueror of death. No problem is too great for him!

## Don't Panic

After ten plagues and numerous confrontations with Pharaoh, Moses led the Israelites out of Egypt. Standing before the Red Sea, the Israelites knew that Pharaoh's army was coming after them. At that moment, their inclination probably was to panic or run, but God commanded, "Do not be afraid. Stand firm and you will see the deliverance the LORD will bring you today. The Egyptians you see today you will never see again. The LORD will fight for you; you need only to be still" (Exod. 14:13). Amazing! As the Egyptians chased them, God simply commanded the Israelites to be still. "Faith," wrote Martin Lloyd-Jones, "is a refusal to panic."[7] Rather than panic, the Israelites "passed through the Red Sea as on dry land; but when the Egyptians tried to do so, they were drowned" (Heb. 11:29).

What are you panicking about? Test results. Mortgage payments. Children's health. Job security. Broken relationships. Trust him and rely on his power. Just as he intervened when thousands of armed soldiers charged the Israelites, he can intervene in your situation.

Imagine Moses standing before the Red Sea. If the people crossed the Red Sea in one night, they couldn't go in a narrow line. With one to three million people, the line would've been eight hundred miles long and taken thirty-five days and nights to cross. The dry land the people walked on had to be three miles wide for them to get through.

According to the quartermaster general of the army, Moses needed 15,000 tons of food each day to feed the people. That's two freight trains, each a mile long. Not to mention that they needed 4,000 tons of firewood to cook food each day (and firewood can't be easy to find in a desert). They also needed water. Eleven million gallons a day to drink and wash a few dishes. That equals a freight train, with tank cars, 1,800 miles long. Each time the Israelites camped, the campground's size was two-thirds the size of Rhode Island, a total of 750 square miles. Do you think Moses had this all figured out when he made the choice of faith? Often God calls us to tasks we cannot do without him. Moses learned that God's power begins where our power ends!

## God's Power

My first car was a Buick Skylark I inherited from my sister. Like most people, I put my first car through a lot. The Skylark's starter malfunctioned, causing me to push-start the car everywhere—across parking lots, out of driveways, on streets. I knew every elevated place in the city, because if I was going downhill I could pop the clutch and start the car easily. Otherwise, I could not do it alone.

Our temptation is to attempt to push-start our lives alone when we feel weak. We push and push and pop the clutch, but nothing happens. Or maybe we recruit some helpful friends, but find we need a power source greater than ourselves. We don't have to pop the clutch to jump-start our lives. God's power accessed by faith is enough!

Paul writes of God's "incomparably great power for us who believe. That power is like the working of his mighty strength, which he exerted in Christ when he raised him from the dead and seated him at his right hand in the heavenly realms" (Eph. 1:19–20). The same power that guided Moses on his journey, that raised Jesus Christ from the dead two thousand years ago, is available for our lives right now. Ask God for the power you need. Admit that you can't do it on your own. Acknowledge that God is bigger than your problems. Remember that he took care of Moses and the Israelites.

Moses lived an amazing life, but he was not perfect. He stuttered. He lost his temper. He murdered. He made bad leadership decisions. But through it all, he learned faith and trust. He walked with God.

We don't have to lead millions of people in order to live extraordinarily. We must simply follow God in daily choices of faith. We must trust his will over our own.

Moses and the Israelites crossed the Red Sea safely, but because of their lack of faith they did not get to enter the Promised Land immediately. The entire generation of Israelites died in the desert except two. Though God did not allow Moses to lead the people into the land, he did allow him to see it. Moses climbed Mount Nebo and looked across the land flowing with milk and honey.

Martin Luther King Jr. called up images of Moses' experience on Mount Nebo when he thundered:

> "I have been to the mountaintop. . . . [God's] allowed me to go up to the mountain, and I've looked over, and I've seen the promised land. I may not get there with you. But I want you to know tonight that we, as a people, will get to the promised land. So I'm happy tonight. I'm not fearing anything. . . . Mine eyes have seen the glory of the coming of the Lord."[8]

After speaking those words, Martin Luther King Jr. returned to his hotel, where he was assassinated. Moses also died on the borders of the Promised Land. But for each of them, the ultimate promised land, the "city with foundations, whose architect and builder is God," awaited (Heb. 11:10).

Deuteronomy contains this eulogy to Moses:

> Since then, no prophet has risen in Israel like Moses, whom the LORD knew face to face, who did all those miraculous signs and wonders the LORD sent him to do in Egypt—to Pharaoh and to all his officials and to his whole land. For no one has ever shown the mighty power or performed the awesome deeds that Moses did in the sight of all Israel.
>
> DEUTERONOMY 34:10–12

## Choose God's Will

Moses' life teaches us that the choices of faith are not always easy or convenient. But they are always worth it.

115

Discovering God's will can be frustrating and confusing, but God never plays games.

So how do we discover God's will? God's ultimate will is that we grow in a relationship with him through Jesus Christ. God's moral will refers to the moral commands and values God communicated in Scripture. God's specific will for each one of us is the area we struggle with most. God's specific will does not contradict his ultimate or moral will. Moses' parents understood they were to protect the life of their boy because anything less would've been outside of God's moral will.

As you consider God's specific will for an area of your life, ask yourself these questions:

1. Am I putting God's desire ahead of my own (Matt. 6:23)?
2. Will it help me to love God and others more (Matt. 22:37–39)?
3. How does this action relate to my personal involvement in fulfilling Christ's Great Commission (Matt. 28:18–20)?
4. Will this help me lead a more holy life (1 Pet. 1:15)?
5. Will this course of action increase my personal knowledge of Christ (2 Pet. 3:18)?
6. Can I be thankful whatever the results or however it works out (1 Thess. 5:18)?[9]

These questions form a strong criteria in helping us determine God's will. They serve as a grid to help us align with God's Word and agenda. When we live God's way and choose his will, we are filled with "an inexpressible and glorious joy," for we are receiving the goal of our faith—the salvation of our souls (1 Pet. 1:8–9).

Real blessing results from surrendering our will to God. On the day I made that lonely drive home from Albuquerque, I had no idea how good life would eventually be. My dreams had disappeared, but God replaced those dreams with ones that fit my personality and gifts better than any others had. Choose God's road—you won't regret it. As Frost concludes:

> Two roads diverged in a wood, and I—
> I took the one less traveled by,
> And that has made all the difference.

I am so thankful I chose God's will. Imagine me today in spandex, playing eighties rock and roll, and you'll be thankful too! His will has made all the difference in my life; it made all the difference in Moses' life; and it can make all the difference in your life.

117

# SEVEN

# A FAITH THAT TRANSFORMS

*It is only by living completely in this world that one learns to have faith.*[1]

DIETRICH BONHOEFFER

In his book *The Kingdom of God Is a Party,* Tony Campolo shares his experience while in Honolulu for a speaking engagement. Because of the time difference from the East Coast, he found himself roaming the streets in the middle of the night, looking for a place to eat. When he located a hole-in-the-wall diner, he entered and took a seat on a stool. As Tony munched his doughnut and sipped his coffee, eight or nine prostitutes entered. Two sat on each side of him, talking to each other in a loud, proud, and crude way. He felt totally out of place. Preparing to leave, he heard one woman say, "Tomorrow's my birthday. I'm going to be thirty-nine."

"So what do you want from me?" one of her companions fired back sarcastically. "A birthday party? What do you want? Ya want me to get you a cake and sing 'Happy Birthday'?"

The woman responded, "Come on! Why do you have to be so mean? I was just telling you, that's all. Why do you have to put me down? I was just telling you it was my birthday. I don't want anything from you. I mean, why should you give me a birthday party? I've never had a birthday party in my whole life. Why should I have one now?"

In that moment, an idea hit Campolo. He waited until the prostitutes left and then asked Harry, the person behind the counter, "Do they come here every night?"

"Yeah," Harry replied.

"The one right next to me, does she come here every night?" Campolo inquired.

"Yeah," he said. "That's Agnes. Yeah, she comes in here every night. Why d'ya wanna know?"

"I heard her say that tomorrow is her birthday. What say you and I do something about that? What do you think about us throwing a birthday party for her—right here—tomorrow night?"

Harry loved the idea. Campolo agreed to show up at 2:30 A.M. to decorate, while Harry and his wife insisted on making the cake. The word got out on the streets, and by 3:15 A.M. the diner was filled with prostitutes. At 3:30 A.M. Agnes walked in with a friend. "Happy Birthday!" everyone screamed.

Campolo writes, "Never have I seen a person so flabbergasted . . . so stunned . . . so shaken. Her mouth fell open.

Her legs seemed to buckle a bit. Her friend grabbed her arm to steady her. As she was led to sit on one of the stools along the counter, we all sang 'Happy Birthday' to her."

When they brought the cake out, Agnes cried. They encouraged her to cut the cake, but she just couldn't do it. She had never received a cake before. Overwhelmed, she asked to keep the cake and take it home. Carrying it toward the door like a religious icon, she promised to return in a few minutes.

In the eerie silence that followed, Campolo looked at the room filled with prostitutes and said, "What do you say we pray." He prayed for Agnes and her friends. He prayed that God's love would touch their hearts. In essence, he prayed that they would join the party celebrating God's grace.

When he finished, Harry said, "Hey! You never told me you were a preacher. What kind of church do you belong to?"

Campolo writes, "In one of those moments when just the right words came, I answered, 'I belong to a church that throws birthday parties for whores at 3:00 in the morning.'"

Harry paused a moment and then said, "No you don't. There's no church like that. If there was, I'd join it. I'd join a church like that."[2]

I daresay much of the world would join a church like that. And that is the kind of church Jesus came to bring. He was continually accused of hanging around with society's riffraff—prostitutes, tax collectors, sinners. He knew that through faith God can transform the worst sinners. He can take a prostitute like Agnes and touch her with his love.

Several thousand years ago, another woman of the night experienced God's love. Her name was Rahab. In Greek, she was a *pornee;* in English, a hooker. She willingly sold herself to anyone with cash. She was not part of the spiritually elite, not a power player in her time, and she lived a rough life. She knew what it meant to be wounded and hurt. She was, like most of the world, broken.

But Rahab's life teaches that God's love can change a broken person. He can transform a prostitute into a princess. Augustine said, "Love slays what we have been that we may be what we were not."[3] Just as God's love transformed Noah into a sailor, Abraham into the father of many nations, Moses into a leader, and Rahab into a princess, he can transform us by grace through faith.

Grace forms the beginning and the end of faith's transformation. God's grace allows us to start our spiritual journey and his grace sustains us to the end of that journey. I learned this lesson when wrestling with doubt. At one difficult point, I struggled with God and meaning in life. Then one night I went to a church service, and someone gave a simple testimony about how God's power changed his life.

As I listened, I realized that the bottom line was that I was a broken, sinful person and that the greatest proof I had for God's existence was myself. God literally put me back together. When I felt worthless, he gave me worth. When I was empty, he filled my soul. When I was dead, he gave me life. Without his grace, I would be nowhere. "Nothing lasts but the grace of God on which I stand," sang Keith Green, and I have found that to be true. That grace is the underlying consistency to all that I am. His grace has brought me safe this far, and grace will carry me home.

Rahab knew something of that grace, and it made her life extraordinary. Extraordinary lives do not necessarily come from righteous legacies. They are often filled with deep scars and dark pasts. But the common denominator that unites us all is God's amazing grace.

Hebrews tells us, "By faith the walls of Jericho fell, after the people had marched around them for seven days. By faith the prostitute Rahab, because she welcomed the spies, was not killed with those who were disobedient" (Heb. 11:30–31). Rahab is the last person to receive commentary in the hall of faith. Incredibly, she is a Gentile, a prostitute, and a woman! What a testimony to the scandal of God's grace and love. Before looking at Rahab's life, let's look at the context of the story of Joshua and the Israelites taking Jericho.

## Faith's Battle

By faith, Hebrews says, the walls of Jericho fell. Jericho was a city located strategically near the mouth of the Jordan River and its walls were engineered to withstand the most intense enemy attack. In this period of history, some city walls were wide enough to drive two chariots side by side across the top.[4] Jericho's huge walls towered over the landscape.

Forty years had passed since the one to three million Israelites crossed the Red Sea with Moses. They should have crossed the Jordan River within forty weeks after crossing the Red Sea, but due to their lack of faith, God had them wander in the desert. The first generation of Israelites, who crossed with Moses, died in the desert. Now the new generation had a new leader, Joshua.

To cross the Jordan River and take the Promised Land, the Israelites had to go through Jericho. According to

123

archaeological records, Jericho is "the earliest fortified town known to scholarship."[5] Its inhabitants thought it would never fall.

What do you suppose the Israelites thought? I suspect many things went through their minds—fear, wonder, excitement. But if a military commander had seen them, he would've laughed—they didn't have a chance. They needed to work, train, and be ready to fight. But God had other things in mind.

God commanded the Israelites:

> "March around the city once with all the armed men. Do this for six days. Have seven priests carry trumpets of rams' horns in front of the ark. On the seventh day, march around the city seven times, with the priests blowing the trumpets. When you hear them sound a long blast on the trumpets, have all the people give a loud shout; then the wall of the city will collapse and the people will go up, every man straight in."
>
> JOSHUA 6:3–5

This was not a normal battle. When I think of ancient battles, I think of the movie *Braveheart*. I see dirty, grimy guys charging with all their might and yelling "Freedom!" Blood and flesh are everywhere, and I hear the sounds of swords clashing and people crying. Yet at the climax of this story, God commands the Israelites to walk around the city seven times, shout, and watch the walls crumble. No charging maniacs with swords, no battering ram, just faith in God's command.

"I'm all for the life of faith," I can imagine an Israelite saying, "but come on, this is absurd."

"Religion has its place, but this is war."

"You don't fight a war by walking around a place in silence."

But the text gives no hint of this kind of talk. The people did not question God's command. After all, they had spent forty years in the desert, listening to their parents tell them, "When God tells you to do something, you do it." Consider the faith it took to march in silence around the strongest fortified city of the day and then to play instruments, shout, and believe the walls would crumble!

They marched around the city out of arrow range, of course, but surely they could hear the taunting of Jericho's army. I suspect there were plenty of jokes shouted down at them as they marched. The VeggieTales version of the fall of Jericho, *Josh and the Big Wall*, portrays Jericho's army chanting, "Keep walking, but you won't knock down that wall. Keep walking, but it isn't gonna fall. It's plain to see that your brains are very small. . . ."

In spite of the taunting, the Israelites leaned on God's strength, power, and wisdom. On the seventh day, as the trumpets blared, they let out a huge cry. Miraculously, the city's walls collapsed. What an amazing move of God!

Have you ever faced difficult odds that towered like Jericho walls? At times, my Jericho walls have been my own insecurities and lack of confidence. Other times, my walls have been difficult people with whom I needed to work things out. My walls also have been constructed of unforgiveness, and I have had to come clean with God and others about my attitude. Through it all, I have discovered that acknowledging my Jericho walls to God provides direction and wisdom. He brings the walls down according to his plan and timing, but I have to take the risk of acknowledging them before God and acting on his Word.

The Israelites took a risk on God, and he moved powerfully. John MacArthur writes:

> There is the type of faith that *receives*, as when we come empty-handed to Christ for salvation. There is the type of faith that *reckons*, that counts on God to undertake for us. There is the faith that *risks*, that moves out in God's power, daring to do the impossible. And there is faith that *rests*, the kind that, in the middle of pain and suffering and rejection, sits back in confidence that God will deliver.[6]

The Israelites learned to risk with unwavering trust. To march around the city, the laughingstock of Jericho, and to believe that God would do what he said took great faith.

When God calls us to a risky task, the safest place on earth is in the middle of that risk. The most dangerous place is the sideline, outside of God's will. If there is no risk, there is no reward. Enoch took a risk when he preached God's judgment. Noah took a risk when he built a boat without seeing the rain. Abraham took a risk when he placed his boy on the altar. Amram and Jochebed took a risk when they pushed their baby down the Nile. Moses took a risk when he stood before Pharaoh. When we share our faith with a friend, take a moral stance at work, defend those who cannot defend themselves, we take risks of faith. These may be small, but they are risks nonetheless.

I remember going off the high dive for the first time. As I climbed the ladder, my heart felt like it was exploding. My palms felt sticky and wet. Adrenaline, excitement, and fear filled me at the thought of doing something new. When I am spiritually bored, this is usually a result of no longer stepping out on the diving board and taking faith-based risks. My faith stagnates because I want the privileges of faith without the risk of faith. I want the blessings of faith without the patience of faith. I want the assurance of faith without the insecurity of things unseen. But "hope that is seen is no hope at all" (Rom. 8:24). A. W. Tozer writes, "God is looking for those through whom he can do the impossible. What a pity that we only attempt that which we can do by ourselves."[7]

The Israelites stepped out in faith. They risked their lives in obedience to God and experienced victory. Faith's battle is God's battle, but victory rarely comes without risk.

## Courageous Faith

Jericho's walls fell as the Israelites moved with courage and faith. But not all the faith was outside the walls of the city—an amazing act of faith occurred inside the walls. When Jericho's walls collapsed, one small section remained standing. It was the home of Rahab, one of the city's riffraff, "for the house she lived in was part of the city wall" (Josh. 2:15).

Earlier, the Israelites had sent two spies to check out Jericho. The spies took every precaution. They carefully disguised themselves to look like natives and approached the city. (Picture this scene with "Mission Impossible" background music.) They arrived and quickly attempted to blend in, then went to the home of a prostitute named Rahab. Visiting prostitutes was a common practice of traveling merchants, so the spies hoped to lay low at Rahab's without being suspect. But someone saw them enter the city and go to Rahab's place. A message was sent to the king of Jericho that spies had entered Rahab's house.

127

The Israelites' identity became known, the word was out, and the authorities were notified. Everything fell apart. Would the spies die here? Would they be tortured for information? If they went further into the city, they would be caught. If they went through the window, they would be run down on the plain.

In this desperate moment, help came from the most unexpected place—the faith of a Gentile prostitute! The king's people came to Rahab's house and asked about the Israelites. Rahab's developing faith was on the line. What would she do? Whom would she trust? If she was caught in a lie, she could die.

Rahab said, "'Yes, the men came to me, but I did not know where they had come from'" (Josh. 2:4). She was a clever woman. She couldn't deny the fact that they had been there, so she played it up. "'At dusk, when it was time to close the city gate, the men left. I don't know which way they went'" (Josh. 2:5). She thought on her feet. Many people come and go at night, so how could she know which way they went?

"Go after them quickly," Rahab said. "You may catch them." She must have struggled not to smile as she gave them the oldest line there is: "They went thataway!"[8] Remember, we are not talking about a person who went to Sunday school and was baptized at age eight. She had not done devotions every morning since she could remember. She was a prostitute, but she was changing. She put her life on the line to save the people of God.

We risk according to the value something has in our lives. On a hiking trek with my friend John Ketchen, I learned this lesson. One night as we were cooking dinner, a black bear came out from the woods. We all ran to the fenced Adirondack shack. The bear roamed around a while and then decided to snatch up John's bag, which contained his journal, book, and pen. Before we knew what was happening, John charged out from the shack and rushed the bear. Shouting, he picked up rocks and pelted the animal. Shocked that a human was charging him, the bear dropped the bag and ran for the woods. When John returned with his bag, he simply said, "Nobody messes with my books." We chanted, "You're the man!"

John's items in that bag were valuable enough for him to take a major risk to get them back. Without even thinking, he went for it. Just like Rahab went for it when her faith was on the line. She risked it all for her family and for God's people.

## Coming to Faith

So how did Rahab develop her faith? In her line of work, she housed many traveling merchants, and from them she heard of God's works, of how the Israelites crossed the Red Sea on dry land and ate bread from heaven. She may have understood the Israelite's high ethical code. I imagine by the time the spies showed up, she was fed up with her life. She felt tired of guilt, tired of being mistreated. She was spiritually hungry and ready for faith.

After diverting the king's men, Rahab went on the roof, where she had hid the spies, and offered an incredible statement of faith:

"I know that the LORD has given this land to you and that a great fear of you has fallen on us, so that all who live in this country are melting in fear because of you. We have heard how the LORD dried up the water of the Red Sea for

129

you when you came out of Egypt, and what you did to Sihon and Og, the two kings of the Amorites east of the Jordan, whom you completely destroyed. When we heard of it, our hearts melted and everyone's courage failed because of you, for the LORD your God is God in heaven above and on the earth below."

JOSHUA 2:9–11

For hundreds of years, the walls of Jericho had stood strong and immovable, a tribute to the city's strength and tenacity. It's no wonder the inhabitants thought the city was invincible. But Rahab had heard of God, and she placed her faith in him. She made a deal with the spies: When they returned to take the city, they would spare her and her family. They told her to hang a scarlet cloth outside her window. Rahab was about to experience grace.

Grace, Anne Lamott writes,

> is unearned love—the love that goes before, that greets us on the way. It's the help you receive when you have no bright ideas left, when you are empty and desperate and have discovered that your best thinking and most charming charm have failed you. Grace is the light or electricity or juice or breeze that takes you from that isolated place and puts you with others who are as startled and embarrassed and eventually grateful as you are to be there.[9]

The spies must have been startled, embarrassed, and grateful to find themselves saved by a Gentile prostitute, but no more surprised than Rahab, who began to follow their God.

When the spies returned to Joshua, they reported what happened. All the people were greatly encouraged by the miraculous deliverance of the spies. Rahab's faith not only

130

encouraged others, but also resulted in her physical, and ultimately spiritual, salvation. After Jericho's walls collapsed,

> Joshua said to the two men who had spied out the land, "Go into the prostitute's house and bring her out and all who belong to her, in accordance with your oath to her." So the young men who had done the spying went in and brought out Rahab, her father and mother and brothers and all who belonged to her. They brought out her entire family and put them in a place outside the camp of Israel.
>
> Then they burned the whole city and everything in it, but they put the silver and gold and the articles of bronze and iron into the treasury of the LORD's house. But Joshua spared Rahab the prostitute, with her family and all who belonged to her, because she hid the men Joshua had sent as spies to Jericho—and she lives among the Israelites to this day.
>
> JOSHUA 6:22–25

Rahab's journey did not end at the city walls. She lived with the Israelites the rest of her life and even married Salmon, a great prince of Judah! Even more amazing, the Gospel of Matthew reveals that Rahab is in the direct lineage of Jesus Christ! God took a prostitute and transformed her into a princess.

## The Scandal of Grace

We can never tell where faith may be found. Jesus said to the religious leaders of his day,

> "I tell you the truth, the tax collectors and the prostitutes are entering the kingdom of God ahead of you. For John came to you to show you the way of righteousness, and you did not believe him, but the tax collectors and the

131

prostitutes did. And even after you saw this, you did not repent and believe him."

MATTHEW 21:31–32

Everyone can come to faith. No one is too high; no one is too low. God's grace is not just amazing, it is scandalous.

Jeffery Dahmer murdered seventeen people. When the police searched his apartment, they found eleven corpses. Dahmer mutilated people and ate their body parts. He did things which are unthinkable. Max Lucado writes of what disturbs him most about Jeffrey Dahmer—not his acts, trial, or punishment, but his conversion. "Months before an inmate murdered him, Jeffrey Dahmer became a Christian" writes Lucado.

> Said he repented. Was sorry for what he did. Profoundly sorry. Said he put his faith in Christ. Was baptized. Started life over. Began reading Christian books and attending chapel. Sins washed. Soul cleansed. Past forgiven. That troubles me. It shouldn't, but it does. Grace for a cannibal?[10]

Indeed, God's grace extends to those on the lowest rung of the ladder, to the Rahabs, the Agneses, and the Dahmers of the world. I, too, am part of the scandal. As I look into my own heart, I realize how desperately I need God's grace. I am thankful his grace is scandalous enough to include everyone—rich and poor, tall and short, righteous and unrighteous, strange and not so strange, smart and not so smart.

Someone once called a church where I ministered a "church for rejects." I think she meant this as an insult, but I thanked her profusely for the greatest of compliments. Jesus saves rejects. He did not come to seek and save the found; he came for the lost, the broken, and the hurting. He described his mission this way: "He has sent me to proclaim freedom for the prisoners and recovery of sight for the blind, to release the oppressed, to proclaim the year of the Lord's favor" (Luke 4:18–19). "Oppressed" literally means "broken to pieces." Jesus brings healing and grace to the broken and the wounded. By dying on the cross for our sins, he has provided a way for the riffraff to enter the kingdom of heaven!

## Bill's Transformation

Bill Fox was transformed by the scandal of God's grace. Bill lived a rough life in his first thirty-nine years. At age ten, he came home and found his sister crying. A beer can and a butcher knife covered in blood sat near the sink. His mother had stabbed his father while he slept. A week later, Bill watched as his mom tenderly rebandaged his father's wound. He never forgot what his father said that day: "It's okay, Bill, she was drunk." This became Bill's excuse for the next three decades.

Bill was arrested for drinking and driving without a license at age thirteen. At age seventeen, he married his pregnant girlfriend and joined the army. Eighteen months later, she took his son and left him. Bill drowned his pain in the bottle. For the next twenty years, he drank every day and partied every night. He was a biker, a drug dealer, and a user. When he kept a job, he lived from paycheck to paycheck. He feared not being a real man, feared not pleasing his dad, feared not being good enough for someone to love. He loved to start fights to prove he was not afraid.

On November 15, 1989, Bill's dad was murdered. Nine months later, his mom died of alcoholism. In between these tragedies, Bill got another divorce. He remembers sitting on the back porch of his rented house and asking God if they were even, since God had taken everyone who loved him away. Then he went back in the house and shot up some cocaine.

Learning about God through Alcoholics Anonymous, Bill finally decided to turn his life over to God, but he knew little about him. Eventually, he found a minister who knew about addiction and who advised Bill to read the Bible to learn more about God. Bill read the four Gospels in two days. He didn't fully understand what he had read, but he was on a mission to know God and to be free from addiction. His faith began to develop. On Easter Sunday, 1995, I baptized Bill as a Christian.

Since then, Bill has steadily grown as a person and as a disciple of Jesus. He recently married Tamy, a wonderful Christian lady. God's call on Bill's life is to share his hope with everyone. He does that through working in the prisons and through working with addicts. He lives extraordinarily as part of the scandal of God's grace.

## Transforming Faith

What do we learn from Rahab's transforming faith?

*God meets us where we are.* Rahab was not perfect when she acted in faith, but God accepted her where she was. God will meet us in a BMW at a plush resort or in an old Ford Pinto outside the Motel 6. He will meet us in the penthouse suite or on a cold, lonely street corner. He will meet us in the deepest, darkest place of sin or in the bright open spaces of righteousness. He will meet us where we are, but he will not leave us there. He will challenge, convict, and empower us to change until we begin to be transformed into the likeness of Christ. That is his pleasure and purpose.

*Taking risks is the safest way to live.* Rahab's life reminds us that without risk there is no victory. When she stuck her neck out, she saved herself, her family, and God's spies. Don't be afraid to take risks for God. The safest place on earth is a risky situation that God has orchestrated.

The difference faith makes in our lives is tremendous. Bill Fox used to start his day with a drink; now he starts it with this prayer: "God, I offer myself to you to do with me as you will. Relieve me of the bondage of self that I might better serve you. Take away my difficulties, that my victory over them will bear witness to those I should show your love, power, and way of life. May I do your will always."[11] God's love transformed Bill just as it transformed Rahab and me. He met us where we were and crowned us with love and compassion.

"Amazing grace, how sweet the sound, that saved a wretch like me."

# EIGHT

# A FAITH THAT GOES THE DISTANCE

*We are not travel agents handing out brochures to places we have never visited. We are faith-explorers of a country without borders, one we discover little by little not to be a place but a person.[1]*

BRENNAN MANNING

Brandon Slay's kneepads reveal volumes. Written with permanent marker on the inside are "Psalm 144:1" and "Joshua 1:9." These are more than just Bible verses to this Olympic wrestler, they are cries of his heart. "Praise be to the LORD my Rock," reads Psalm 144:1, "who trains my hands for war, my fingers for battle"; "Have I not commanded you?"

asks God in Joshua 1:9. "Be strong and courageous. Do not be terrified; do not be discouraged, for the LORD your God will be with you wherever you go." With this faith, Slay walked out onto the Olympic wrestling mat in Sydney, Australia, an unknown.

Slay was so unknown the critics didn't even bother to mention him. The programs at the Olympics mistakenly omitted Slay's name and listed Joe Williams, whom he beat in the national finals. The few who did know who Slay was said he was lucky to have won the national tournament. They claimed he barely inched by to win the Olympic trials and that he would do nothing at the Olympics.

But the world did a double take in Sydney when Slay beat Bouvaisar Saitiev of Russia. Saitiev had been undefeated for six years and was picked as the best wrestler in the world for his weight division. Slay said, "When Saitiev went down, it was one of the most amazing feelings in my life, athletically. It was pure exuberance, like someone set off bottle-rockets inside my body. You just can't control yourself. It's amazing."[2]

Slay went all the way to the 76kg freestyle Olympic gold medal match on September 30. His opponent was Alexander Leipold of Germany. He lost the match on points and was awarded the silver medal, but he gained something worth far more than gold.

Slay's face lights up when he talks about it. "You learn more from losing than from winning. You learn more from trudging through valleys than from scaling peaks. The silver taught me that in life things are going to happen. We can either blame God and others, choose to be angry for years, or get over it and move on. I learned that losing in life doesn't come from losing but from missing out on the learning, growth, and challenges that lie ahead. I learned that joy doesn't come from winning or losing."[3] For Slay, joy begins and ends with Jesus Christ. These lessons profoundly impacted his life in the weeks following the Olympics. But what Slay didn't know then was that he would see his silver turn to gold.

In the October following the Olympics, the press announced that Leipold had tested positive for steroids and that Slay might receive the gold medal. Slay learned of the official decision to give him the gold while he was driving through Sunray, Texas. He feels the name is a beautiful description for both his faith and that phone call. That day, his whole life changed. On November 15 Slay received the gold medal on the *Today* show in New York.

Through it all, he learned what it means to live with second place, to struggle, to keep going, and ultimately to achieve gold. He claims that the real path to victory is to give one's whole life to God. "God is related and involved in every aspect of my life. I would not be where I am today without his gifts, grace, and mercy. I am totally weak without him. To go the distance in faith you have to realize that you can't do this on your own. You have to surrender to God. Relax your soul. Relax your mind. Relax your heart. Give it up to him."[4]

The name of Slay's athletic ministry captures his experience: Greater Gold. He uses sports, wrestling camps, and all-sports camps to further God's kingdom. "When I say greater gold, I mean that there is a greater gold to life. The greatest gold medal you can have in life is having Jesus Christ in your heart."[5]

Slay says the most important thing is not how you start, but how you finish. "Life isn't about one defining moment," he says. "Whether you've lost your loved one or you've won Olympic gold, life is about the journey we take. Not the gold medal, not the fact that you've endured a horrible circumstance; life is about the marathon, not a sprint."[6]

Anyone can start a marathon, but it takes patience, courage, and endurance to finish one. In the life of faith, God does not call us to simply start; he calls us to finish. He challenges us to press forward in difficult circumstances, to continue through pain, hardship, victories, and losses. And we achieve moments of silver and moments of gold until we cross the finish line. "Therefore," reads Hebrews, "since we are surrounded by such a great cloud of witnesses, let us throw off everything that hinders and the sin that so easily entangles, and let us run with perseverance the race marked out for us" (Heb. 12:1).

"Remember those who have gone before you," the author of Hebrews says. "Be encouraged to finish the race. Don't quit! Don't stop!" Hebrews 11 challenges us to look at the lives of the faithful, but chapter 12 says *they* are witnessing *us*. Picture a huge stadium filled with people. Across the ring of honor are the names of those who have gone before: Abel, Enoch, Noah, Abraham, Moses, Rahab, and others. They are cheering you on to run the race of faith, all the way to the finish line. *The Message* translates this passage, "Do you see what this means—all these pioneers who blazed the way, all these veterans cheering us on? It means we'd better get on with it. Strip down, start running—and never quit!" (Heb. 12:1 MESSAGE).

Remember Abel and his legacy of faith. He worshiped God authentically from his heart, and he still speaks even though he is dead. He challenges us to live with the end in mind. Remember Enoch and the way he walked with

140

God. He placed his faith and trust in the unseen God and did not suffer death. Remember Noah, whose faith overcame all doubt. He built an ark to protect his family during the flood. He cultivated a faith that withstood the most devastating storm. Remember Abraham, who followed God's vision without knowing where he was going. He waited twenty-four years for the child God had promised. Then, in the ultimate test of faith, he was willing to sacrifice that child. Remember Moses, who lived for God and refused to be known as the son of Pharaoh's daughter. He placed more value on the treasures of Christ than the treasures of the world. He chose God's will over his own and fulfilled God's purpose. Remember Rahab, who took a risk and experienced God's amazing grace.

Continue in faith with the memory of those who have gone before. They served as God's ambassadors, even when it hurt. Their everyday faith led to extraordinary lives.

## Reaching the Finish Line

Many start the life of faith like they are running a sprint. But soon they wear out and give up. Maybe doubt overtakes their faith, and they choose not to dig deeper for truth. Perhaps their family members and friends pressure them, and they fall back into a lifestyle of sin and addiction. More often than not, they slowly stop growing and then drift. We must remember that finishing well is more important than starting well.

In 1968 the Olympics was held in Mexico City. One of the featured events was the grueling, twenty-six-mile marathon. That year, the competitors ran hard and long until they finally entered the Olympic stadium and crossed the finish line. There were crowds, cameras, and hoopla. By 7:00 P.M., however, the temperature was cooling and the skies were darkening. Over an hour after Mamo Waldi of Ethiopia had taken first place, an injured runner wearing the colors of Tanzania entered the stadium. He was in pain and moving slowly, but his eyes were firmly set on the finish line. John Steven Aquari was his name, and he had taken a bad fall earlier but continued on in spite of a bandaged, bloody leg. Those left in the stadium began to stand, cheer, and clap for this lone runner who struggled for the finish line. One foot in front of the other, he eventually finished the race.

Later, in the dressing room, the man was approached by curious reporters who wondered why he kept on running. Why did he finish the race, knowing it had been won a long time before? Why finish, knowing he would not secure a medal? His response to the interviewers was profound: "My country did not send me seven thousand miles to start this race. My country sent me to finish."

God has called us not only to start the race of faith, but to finish. At times the race is downhill and we feel power and confidence. We sense God's blessing in our lives. We are aware of his Spirit guiding us. We see fruit from our labors and abide in Christ effortlessly. But at other times we feel like we can do no more than place one foot in front of the other. Problems weigh us down. Doubt trips us up. Heartache steals our motivation. In those times, God draws even closer to us, sustaining us and empowering us to take the next step.

If you feel like the finish line is unreachable, focus on taking the next step. You *will* sprint again. But for today, it is enough to trudge along. One thing is certain—whether we are sprinting or painfully stumbling along in faith, God desperately loves us and will empower us until we finish. As Paul writes, "He who began a good work in you will carry it on to completion until the day of Christ Jesus" (Phil. 1:6).

## Throw Off Everything That Hinders

In light of the ancient witnesses cheering for us, Hebrews challenges us to "throw off everything that hinders and the sin that so easily entangles" (Heb. 12:1). For runners, any kind of extra weight is a hindrance. One extra pound can mean the difference between winning and losing. In our lives, we have to be willing to cast off everything that hinders, no matter how small. My hindrances may not be inherently evil, but if they weigh me down, they need to go.

We must throw off the sin that so easily entangles. Sin simply means "missing the mark." The original term was used for an archer who fired an arrow but missed the mark for which he aimed. When we sin, we miss God's mark for our lives. Sin hinders us and holds us back from God's purpose.

Most of us have Ph.D.s in sin. We know how we do it. We can be lured into sin through situations. We can sin by intentionally avoiding something God wants for us. We can sin through laziness, by ignoring the needs of others, or through attitudes which are not thankful.

So how do we cast off the sin that hinders? First, we must look honestly at our lives and God's Word. We must recognize where we fall short. And we must not bury, minimize, or rationalize our sins away.

We often blame other people or circumstances, which is perhaps our most natural instinct. After Adam and Eve

143

sinned in the garden, God asked, "Have you eaten from the tree that I commanded you not to eat from?" (Gen. 3:11).

What was Adam's reply? "Yes, Lord, I am very sorry, please forgive me." Not! He said, "The woman you put here with me—she gave me some fruit from the tree and I ate it" (Gen. 3:12). God, my sin was Eve's fault.

Then God turned to Eve and said, "What is this you have done?"

Eve replied, "The serpent deceived me and I ate." My sin was the serpent's fault.

Today, rather than blame our sin on a serpent, we blame DNA. Our sin is the fault of genetics. Consider this *Psychology Today* headline: "NOT GUILTY—Can't Stick to Your Diet, Blame It On Your Genes." Blame it on anything but ourselves. We are not the problem; everybody else is. Society made us do it. We were born this way. The tragedy of this thinking is that it prevents us from moving forward. We cannot progress spiritually until we face our sin and take responsibility.

Second, pray for God's help. God loves for us to pray to him. We cannot deal with sin on our own; we must seek his power and wisdom. Why does God want us to ask for help in dealing with our hindrances? Because he understands. Jesus, the writer of Hebrews reminds us, "had the same temptations we do though he never once gave way to them and sinned. So let us come boldly to the very throne of God and find grace to help us in our time of need" (Heb. 4:16 TLB). Jesus faced temptation like we do. Did Jesus struggle with honesty? Yes. Sexuality? Yes. Hate? Yes. Self-pity? Yes. He had free will, but he never sinned. He overcame sin. C. S. Lewis once claimed that Jesus is the only person in the world who truly knows the power

144

of temptation, because he never succumbed to it. When we give in, we experience a momentary relief. Jesus never knew that relief. So he can help us. But he asks that we come boldly, with no hesitation. Don't be intimidated. Raise your voice to God and cry "Help me!"

Third, change the focus. The way we think determines the way we feel, which in turn determines the way we act. As Samuel Smiles said, "Sow a thought and you reap an act; sow an act and you reap a habit; sow a habit and you reap a character; sow a character and you reap a destiny."[7] Temptation begins with a thought. The battle begins in our minds. The key to overcoming temptation is to refocus our attention. Look at something else, go for a jog, change the scenery, take a cold shower. Do whatever you need to do to shift your focus from the temptation to Jesus.

## Focus on Jesus

The ancients motivate and cheer us on, but the greatest example of all is Jesus. The writer of Hebrews moves from the great cloud of witnesses to the ultimate witness. "Let us fix our eyes on Jesus," Hebrews reads,

> the author and perfecter of our faith, who for the joy set before him endured the cross, scorning its shame, and sat down at the right hand of the throne of God. Consider him who endured such opposition from sinful men, so that you will not grow weary and lose heart.
>
> HEBREWS 12:2–3

I have a picture of an eagle on my office wall. The caption underneath the eagle reads, "Focus. If you chase two rabbits, both will escape." To succeed in life, we must remain focused, otherwise we will give up when times are tough. When we focus on Jesus, we can endure all kinds of difficulties.

Father Maximilian Kolbe was a prisoner at Auschwitz in August, 1941. After a prisoner escaped from the camp, the Nazis ordered that ten prisoners die by starvation. Father Kolbe took the place of one of the condemned men. The Nazis kept Kolbe in the starvation bunker for two weeks and then put him to death by lethal injection on August 14, 1941.

Thirty years later, a survivor of Auschwitz described the effect of Kolbe's action:

> It was an enormous shock to the whole camp. We became aware that someone among us in this spiritual dark night of the soul was raising the standard of love on high. Some-one unknown, like everyone else, tortured and bereft of name and social standing, went to a horrible death for the sake of someone not even related to him. Therefore it is not true, we cried, that humanity is cast down and tram-pled in the mud, overcome by oppressors, and over-whelmed by hopelessness. Thousands of prisoners were convinced the true world continued to exist and that our torturers would not be able to destroy it. To say that Father Kolbe died for us or for that person's family is too great a simplification. His death was the salvation of thousands. . . . We were stunned by his act, which became for us a mighty explosion of light in the dark camp.[8]

Just as those prisoners were changed by Father Kolbe's sacrifice, we are changed by Christ's sacrifice. As I consider all he has done for me, I am overwhelmed with gratitude. He went through pain and death so that I could be in a relationship with God and experience grace. He suffered that I might live. He endured that I might endure. He hurt that I might be healed.

When I focus on Jesus, my attitude is changed. My difficulties don't appear that difficult, nor my suffering that tough. When I take my focus off Jesus, I quickly slip into whining mode. "Woe is me! My schedule is so full. The pressure is so great!" But in light of Christ's endurance, what are my momentary trials? In light of his love and passion, what are my struggles? My complaining and whining are reduced to silence. My attitude takes a whole new direction. I smile more, laugh more, and am filled with more compassion for others. I live in the moment with the end in mind.

## Remember the Cross

P. T. Forsyth said, "Christ is to us just what his cross is. All that Christ was in heaven or on earth was put into what he did there. . . . Christ, I repeat, is to us just what his cross is. You do not understand Christ until you understand his cross."[9]

Imagine Christ's perspective from the cross. He was cursed with tongues and struck with fists he designed. Forced to carry a beam of wood that he, as God, spoke into existence. Led down a path to a hill created by him in ages past.

In his lifetime, he had silenced the roaring thunder and muzzled the raging storm. He had healed the sick and showed control over the spirit world. The dead had risen at his word. But here, he withheld his power to make peace between God and man.

He heard their taunting, "Liar, liar, if you are the Christ then save yourself." Through blood and tears, he saw those around him shaking their heads and wagging their fingers. The disciples slipping off, out of the back of the crowd. His mother's stricken face. He could have shaken the earth into oblivion or called down lightning from the sky. He could have simply stepped down and walked into glory.

From the cross, he saw people like you and me, people that he loved more than life. And then he uttered the words all creation hinges upon. Without these words, the morning would no longer gather, nor the sun set. The proud waves of the sea would no longer halt at their shore, nor moonlight spill across the prairies. There would be no faith, no hope, no love—"Father, forgive them for they know not what they do." What love! Without Jesus' sacrifical death and forgiveness the world would be without hope and would ultimately come to ruin. His mercy reaches out to touch us all. When we focus on him and open our hearts, we cannot help but be transformed.

Jesus suffered and endured because he focused on the "joy set before him" (Heb. 12:2). During Greece's Isthmian games, a pedestal was placed at the finish line. The pedestal held the winner's prize—the wreath. The runners endured agony and pain to win that prize. Jesus, in much the same way, endured all kinds of hardship for the joy of reconciling God and man.

After Jesus endured the cross, Hebrews says he "sat down." The mind-blowing thing about that statement is that Jesus, the great High Priest, did what no other priest would ever dare to do. Priests never sat down; there were no seats in the tabernacle or the temple sanctuaries. A priest's responsibility was to sacrifice, sacrifice, sacrifice. But Jesus offered one sacrifice at the cross and sat down as he said, "It is finished." He did not sit down because he needed a rest. He sat down because his work of redemption was complete; it was an honor to sit.

> God exalted him to the highest place
>     and gave him the name that is above every name,
> that at the name of Jesus every knee should bow,
>     in heaven and on earth and under the earth,
> and every tongue confess that Jesus Christ is Lord
>     to the glory of God the father.
>
> PHILIPPIANS 2:9

He sat at God's right hand as a sign of authority, though he is not literally sitting in a chair. He "lives to intercede" for us before God (Heb. 7:25). He is the "author and perfecter of our faith" (Heb. 12:2). As we focus on all those who have gone before us, including Jesus, we are motivated to continue on in faith.

One of the most powerful movies I have seen is *Saving Private Ryan*. The movie is about a group of World War II GIs who embark on a mission to find Private Ryan. Ryan's three brothers had been killed in the war, and the United States determined that losing three of four sons was enough sacrifice for any mother. So the GIs' mission was to find Ryan and ensure that he safely begin his journey back to America to be reunited with his mother.

The GIs were not excited about this mission. They argued and complained, but orders were orders, so they began to search. Several times they came under fire and some of their team died. Eventually, they found Private Ryan, but they came under enemy fire bringing him back. Captain John

149

Miller (played by Tom Hanks), who led the GIs on the mission, was badly wounded. Private Ryan walked over to him and then looked at the destruction all around him. He looked down at Miller, who was dying. Miller looked up at Ryan and uttered his last words: "Earn this."

In other words, Look at what has been done to rescue you. Look at the lives that have been lost. Look at those who have gone before you and exhibited courage, sacrifice, and faith so that you might live. Go home. Live in light of this. Live with gratitude for this. "Earn this." At the end of his life, Private Ryan revisited their graves. He fell to his knees, weeping, and said, "Tell me I lived a good life."

I have similar sentiments when I look at the lives of the faithful. Consider their incredible courage! They lived their faith no matter the cost. Even though most of them never saw the fulfillment of Jesus' coming, they ran the race to the finish nevertheless. They lived extraordinarily. And they cheer us on to the finish line.

The lives of the ancients bear witness to the power of tide riding. Remember them daily, especially when things get tough. Let God's power, as seen in their lives, motivate and encourage you to carry on. Live in light of their courage, sacrifice, and faith. Live a life worthy of the legacy they pass on. Live as ambassadors on God's faith mission. "Earn this."

Of course, we cannot earn salvation, but we can respond to the faithful with grateful hearts and the everyday faith that leads to extraordinary lives. Then, on the last day as we plead like Private Ryan, "Tell me I lived a good life," God will respond, "Well done, good and faithful servant. Come and share your master's happiness!"

# NOT

## Introduction

1. William James, quoted in Brennan Manning, *The Signature of Jesus* (Sisters, Ore.: Multnomah, 1996), 95.

2. Faith Popcorn and Lys Marigold, *Clicking: 16 Trends to Future Fit Your Life, Your Work, and Your Business* (New York: Harper Collins, 1996), 13.

## Chapter One: *A Faith That Rides Tides*

1. Blaise Pascal, quoted in Bill and Kathy Peel, *Discover Your Destiny* (Colorado Springs: NavPress, 1996), 215.

2. Bruce Thielemann, "Tide Riding," audiotape of a message presented for *Preaching Today* (Carol Stream, Ill.: Preaching Today, 1999). I am indebted to Thielemann's message for the tide-riding metaphor and for the seed ideas for this book.

3. William Shakespeare, *Julius Caesar*, quoted in Bruce Thielemann, "Tide Riding."

4. Quoted in Philip Yancey, *Reaching for the Invisible God* (Grand Rapids: Zondervan, 2000), 70.

5. T. H. Huxley, quoted in Kent Hughes, *Hebrews, Volume Two: An Anchor for the Soul* (Wheaton: Crossway Books, 1993), 60.

6. Ambrose Pierce, quoted in Kent Hughes, *Hebrews, Volume Two: An Anchor for the Soul* (Wheaton: Crossway Books, 1993), 60.

7. Matthew Henry, quoted in Arthur W. Pink, *An Exposition of Hebrews* (Grand Rapids: Baker Books, 1954), 652.

8. Kathleen Norris, *Amazing Grace: A Vocabulary of Faith* (New York: Riverhead Books, 1998), 169.

9. Eveline Rivers, personal interview (Jan. 11, 2001).

10. Oswald Chambers, quoted in *Leadership*, no. 3, vol. 2 (Summer 1981): 40.

11. Sir Francis Drake, quoted in John Maxwell, "Thoughts for the 21st Century," audiotape of a message presented for *Injoy Life Club* (Atlanta: 2000).

## Chapter Two: *A Faith That Leaves a Legacy*

1. Vern E. Smith and Jon Meacham, "The War Over King's Legacy," *The Washington Post.Com* (http://www.washngtonpost.com/wp-srv/national/longterm/mlk/legacy/legacy.html).

2. Chris Tina Leimer, "Tombstone Epitaphs," The Tombstone Traveler's Guide (1996–1999) (http://www.flash.net/~liemer/ epitaph.html).

3. The story is true, but Thomas Dowling's name is fictitious.

4. Thomas Dowling, personal interview (Jan. 4, 2001).

5. Ibid.

6. Ibid.

7. Ibid.

8. Ibid.

9. Scholars have argued over whether or not God's displeasure centered around the type of offering. Abel brought a blood offering; Cain brought a fruit offering. Both types of offerings were accepted by God in the Old Testament, but the Old Testament sacrificial laws were not established at this time. There is a theme in Genesis of the ground being cursed. After Adam and Eve ate from the tree of the knowledge of good and evil, God said to Adam, "Cursed is the ground because of you; through painful toil you will eat of it all the days of your life" (Gen. 3:17). Maybe Cain's offering was rejected because it came from the ground and was not acceptable at that time. Perhaps God approved of Abel's offering because it was a blood offering, which pointed to the need for sacrifice and forgiveness of sin. Whatever the actual reason for the rejection, I contend that the underlying issue is one of the heart.

10. Jaroslav Pelikan, quoted in Avery Dules, "The Ways We Worship," *First Things* (March 1998): 28–34.

11. A.W. Tozer, quoted in "Reflections," *Christianity Today* 41, no. 5 (April 1997): 70.

12. Leonard Sweet, *Aqua Church* (Loveland, Colo.: Group, 1999), 64.

13. Ted Turner, *People* (June 12, 2000): 62.

14. Stephen Covey, *The 7 Habits of Highly Effective People* (New York: Simon and Schuster, 1989), 96.

15. Ravi Zacharias, *Jesus Among Other Gods: The Absolute Claims of the Christian Message* (Nashville: Word, 2000), 18.

## Chapter Three: *A Faith That Walks with God*

1. Søren Kierkegaard, *The Laughter Is on My Side*, eds. Roger Poole and Henrik Stangerup (Princeton: Princeton University Press, 1989), 69.

2. See Dave Kunst, "The Earthwalker" (http://www.bonus.com/bonus/card/Earthwalk.html).

3. Brennan Manning, *The Ragamuffin Gospel* (Sisters, Ore.: Multnomah, 1990), 31–33.

4. Jerry Adler, "Unbeliever's Quest," *Newsweek* (March 1997): 64–65.

5. George Barna, "Virtual America," *The Barna Report* (1994–1995).

6. Brennan Manning, *The Signature of Jesus* (Sisters, Ore.: Multnomah, 1996), 93–94.

7. Albert Schweitzer, quoted in Leonard Sweet, *A Cup of Coffee at the Soul Café* (Nashville: Broadman & Holman, 1998), 34.

8. R. C. Sproul, *The Holiness of God* (Wheaton: Tyndale, 1998), 25.
9. Ibid., 26.
10. C. S. Lewis, quoted in Edythe Draper, *Draper's Book of Quotations for the Christian World* (Wheaton: Tyndale, 1992), entry 3809.
11. Kierkegaard, *The Laughter Is on My Side*, 73.

## Chapter Four: *A Faith That Obeys God*

1. Catherine Booth, "The 'Army Mother,'" *Christian History* 9, no. 26 (1990): 9.
2. John MacArthur, *Hebrews* (Chicago: Moody, 1983), 320.
3. Ibid, 320.
4. Catherine Booth, "The 'Army Mother,'" 9.
5. James and Gil Farren, personal interview (Jan. 2, 2001).
6. Ibid.
7. Ibid.
8. Ibid.
9. Ibid.
10. Ibid.
11. Ibid.
12. Oswald Chambers, "Run Today's Race," *Christianity Today* 31, no. 17 (December 1985): 35.
13. Quoted in Sweet, *Aqua Church*, 189.
14. I am indebted to John Ortberg for the connection between the three little pigs and Jesus' teaching. See John Ortberg, *Love Beyond Reason* (Grand Rapids: Zondervan, 1998), 80.
15. Dwight L. Moody, *Leadership* 10, no. 4. (Fall 1989): 32.
16. Sweet, *Aqua Church*, 110–12.

## Chapter Five: *A Faith That Follows God's Vision*

1. George Müller, *Leadership* 12, no. 4 (Fall 1991).

2. Rob Maupin, personal interview (Jan. 3, 2001).
3. Ibid.
4. Corrie ten Boom, quoted in Draper, *Draper's Book of Quotations for the Christian World*, entry 3713.
5. I am indebted to John Maxwell for the idea of Abraham crossing boundaries. See John Maxwell, "Big People See the Big Picture," audiotape of a message presented for *Injoy Life Club* (Atlanta: Injoy Life Club, 1992).
6. Manning, *The Signature of Jesus*, 16.
7. Oswald Chambers, quoted in Draper, *Draper's Book of Quotations for the Christian World*, entry 3668.
8. Thomas Merton, *Thoughts in Solitude* (Garden City, N.Y.: Doubleday, 1968), 81.
9. Henri Nouwen, *Sabbatical Journey: The Diary of His Final Year* (New York: Crossroad, 1998), 2.
10. Hughes, *Hebrews*, 108.
11. Anne Lamott, *Traveling Mercies* (New York: Anchor Books, 1999), 28–29.
12. Martin Luther, "Powerful Preaching," *Christian History* 39, no. 3 (1993): 28.
13. Rob Maupin, personal interview.

## Chapter Six: *A Faith That Chooses God's Will*

1. Tom Robbins, quoted in Tom Peters, *The Circle of Innovation* (New York: Vintage, 1997), 167.
2. Paul Little, quoted in Ron Oertli, *The Growing Disciple: The 2:7 Series* (Colorado Springs: NavPress, 1979), 38.
3. Oswald Chambers, quoted in Draper, *Draper's Book of Quotations for the Christian World*, entry 3996.
4. Phillip J. Longman, "The Cost of Children," *U.S. News and World Report*, (March 30, 1998).

5. Malcolm Muggeridge, *Jesus Rediscovered* (Wheaton: Tyndale, 1969), 61.

6. Corrie ten Boom, quoted in Draper, *Draper's Book of Quotations for the Christian World,* entry 5460.

7. Martyn Lloyd-Jones, quoted in Draper, *Draper's Book of Quotations for the Christian World,* entry 3677.

8. Martin Luther King Jr., quoted in Philip Yancey, "Moses, Prince of Israel," *The Prince of Egypt* (Nashville: Thomas Nelson, 1998), 202–203.

9. Oertli, *The Growing Disiple,* 41.

**Chapter Seven: *A Faith That Transforms***

1. Dietrich Bonhoeffer, *Christian History,* no. 4, vol. X (1991): 13.

2. Tony Campolo, *The Kingdom of God Is a Party* (Dallas: Word, 1990), 3–8.

3. St. Augustine, quoted in M. C. D'arcy, *The Mind and Heart of Love* (New York: Henry Holt, 1947), 87.

4. MacArthur, *Hebrews,* 361.

5. Trent C. Butler, *Word Biblical Commentary: Joshua* (Waco: Word, 1983), 32, quoted in Hughes, *Hebrews,* 142.

6. MacArthur, *Hebrews,* 362–63.

7. A. W. Tozer, quoted in Baerg, *Created for Excellence,* (Tacoma, Wash.: Inspiration Ministries, 1996), 114.

8. Liz Curtis Higgs, *Bad Girls of the Bible* (Colorado Springs: WaterBrook Press, 1999), 158.

9. Lamott, *Traveling Mercies,* 139.

10. Max Lucado, *In the Grip of Grace* (Dallas: Word, 1996), 35–36.

11. Bill Fox, personal interview (April, 2000).

**Chapter Eight: *A Faith That Goes the Distance***

1. Manning, *The Signature of Jesus,* 26–27.

2. Brandon Slay, personal interview (Jan. 7, 2001).

3. Ibid.

4. Ibid.

5. Ibid.

6. Ibid.

7. Samuel Smiles, quoted in Draper, *Draper's Book of Quotations for the Christian World,* entry 1041.

8. Tony Campolo, *Let Me Tell You a Story* (Nashville: Word, 2000), 39–40.

9. P. T. Forsyth, quoted in R. C. Sproul, *The Cross of Christ: Study Guide for the Video or Audio Series* (Orlando: Ligonier Ministries, 1989), 12.

**Jud Wilhite** is a teaching pastor on the leadership team of Crossroads Christian Church in Corona, California. He teaches at the Londen Institute for Evangelism and is an adjunct professor for Azusa Pacific University. He and his wife, Lori, have one daughter, Emma.